DELIVERED

Living Free in Days of Oppression

A Flexible Inductive Study of Judges

Pam Gillaspie

Scripture taken from the
NEW AMERICAN STANDARD BIBLE®,
© Copyright 1960, 1962, 1963, 1968, 1971, 1972, 1973, 1975, 1977, 1995
by The Lockman Foundation.
Used by permission. (www.Lockman.org)

Delivered: Living Free in Days of Oppression

Copyright © 2024 by Pam Gillaspie
Published by Ignite Bible Ministries
www.pamgillaspie.com

ISBN 978-1-960938-17-6

Printed in the United States of America

2024

DELIVERED

Living Free in Days of Oppression

Life happens. Whether it's family or church, job or kids, sickness or health, busyness or loneliness, life is filled with unpredictable elements, with variables that lift us up one day only to come crashing down like waves over a ship's bow the next. Life happens.

In the midst of life's happenings, even the best intentions can run aground. Optimism says "Not me!" but we live in a broken world that both theologians and actuaries can tell you will eventually disappoint even the glass-is-half-fulls among us.

Flexible inductive studies are designed with hopeful reality in mind! The main portion of the study offers flexibility enough to bend to each week's demands (and surprises!) and the *Extras!* section at the end of each lesson invites those with different learning styles—and the occasional gift of more time!—to try some new ways of remembering the lesson.

When life happens, don't drop your Bible . . . hold it more tightly and flex!

Enjoy!

HOW TO USE THIS STUDY

Flexible Inductive Studies meet you where you are and take you as far as you want to go.

1. **WEEKLY STUDY:** The main text guides you through the complete topic of study for the week.

2. **FYI boxes:** For Your Information boxes provide bite-sized material to shed additional light on the topic.

3. **ONE STEP FURTHER and other sidebar boxes:** Sidebar boxes give you the option to push yourself a little further. If you have extra time or are looking for an extra challenge, you can try one, all, or any number in between! These boxes give you the ultimate in flexibility.

4. **DIGGING DEEPER boxes:** If you're looking to go further, Digging Deeper sections will help you sharpen your skills as you continue to mine the truths of Scripture for yourself.

CONTENTS

Previously in . . .
The Bible

The Backstory and the Method

In the beginning God created the heavens and the earth.
—Genesis 1:1

Why start a study on the book of Judges in Genesis? Great question!
Here's the short answer: in order to understand the message of Judges,
we need to understand its context—what comes before it, what comes after it, who it was written for and why. We need to pay attention to context
whenever we read the Bible (or anything else for that matter!) or we run
the risk of misunderstanding and misapplying. That's the short answer.

Here's the longer answer that's been the burden of my heart for over 25
years now. Studying any individual portion of the Bible in isolation without having at least a general understanding of the whole often leads to
frustration and failure. As long as I can remember, this has been a problem
for people who are seeking to know the Word of God. Until you reach a
tipping point of knowledge where the people and events start to connect,
the Bible study road can be long and hard.

If You're in a Class

Work on **Week One** together on your first day of class. This will be a great way to start getting to
know each other!

For those who have come to know the accounts of the Bible throughout their childhood, the dots connect much more quickly. For those who sit under regular expositional teaching of God's Word, the base of truth builds.

In recent years, though, simple biblical literacy (think Adam, Eve, Noah, Moses) has declined and the path to basic understanding has become increasingly difficult to find.

So, yes, we will be studying Judges inductively, but instead of starting off there, we are going to take some time to consider what precedes the book of Judges in the Bible as well as look at some "spoilers" to come, specifically how the deliverers in Judges point to mankind's need for an ultimate Deliverer!

Don't Be Overwhelmed!

Take this as an imperative! I'm not much into mandatory—nobody is really—but please, please, please take this instruction seriously. Don't let this study overwhelm you. Occasionally it may "whelm" you. A little whelmed is okay from time to time. A little whelmed challenges us to engage and grow and be strengthened. Overwhelmed though? Overwhelmed almost always paralyzes. Short of paralyzing it sucks joy out of the room. So don't go there. Do what you can and if you feel yourself going under, either slow the pace or reach out to a classmate or friend who can help!

USING AN INDUCTIVE APPROACH

As we study together, we'll use an inductive approach toward the Bible in order to learn to discover truth for ourselves.

Inductive study has three main components that we'll walk through step-by-step: *observation, interpretation,* and *application.*

Observation asks: *What does the text say?*

Interpretation asks: *What does the text mean?*

Application asks: *How can I apply this truth in my life?*

Together they lead to transformation by the Spirit through the Word.

MARKING the text of Scripture is one tool that will help us to observe the text well. We'll identify key words by reading carefully, then we'll mark them. Key words are typically repeated and critical to understanding the meaning of the text. When we identify key words, we're beginning to see what is going on in the text, what the author's main point is. As we mark key words, we ASK the 5W and H questions (*Who? What? When? Where? Why? and How?*).

THE QUICK START SUMMARY

Instead of giving you a summary of the first part of the Bible in my words, let's have God's Word itself bring you up to speed. We'll start with Hebrews 11 which provides a concise one-chapter summary of the Old Testament and points forward to the final, completed work of Jesus! It doesn't mention everyone, but the framework of the whole Bible is in there and so immeasurably helpful! For our purposes today, we'll look just at the first seven verses.

Hebrews 11:1-7

1 *Now faith is the assurance of things hoped for, the conviction of things not seen.*

2 *For by it the men of old gained approval.*

3 *By faith we understand that the worlds were prepared by the word of God, so that what is seen was not made out of things which are visible.*

4 *By faith Abel offered to God a better sacrifice than Cain, through which he obtained the testimony that he was righteous, God testifying about his gifts, and through faith, though he is dead, he still speaks.*

5 *By faith Enoch was taken up so that he would not see death; AND HE WAS NOT FOUND BECAUSE GOD TOOK HIM UP; for he obtained the witness that before his being taken up he was pleasing to God.*

6 *And without faith it is impossible to please Him, for he who comes to God must believe that He is and that He is a rewarder of those who seek Him.*

FOR FUTURE STUDY:

A Big-Picture Guide to the Bible

If you're looking for a more comprehensive yet still speedy way to grasp the Bible's main storyline, check out *Sweeter than Chocolate! Hebrews 11: A Big-Picture Guide to the Bible.*

7 *By faith Noah, being warned* by God *about things not yet seen, in reverence prepared an ark for the salvation of his household, by which he condemned the world, and became an heir of the righteousness which is according to faith.*

DISCUSS with your GROUP or PONDER on your own . . .

What time period does Hebrews 11:1-7 cover?

How did people gain God's approval?

According to Hebrews 11, how can a person please God? How does this compare with common cultural thinking?

Do you try to please God? If so, how are you going about it? How does it line up with Hebrews 11?

How does the author of Hebrews define faith? What can we learn from the examples of faith he provides?

What examples of faith have you seen firsthand? How have they affected your thinking and behavior?

The Need for a Deliverer . . .

From its earliest chapters, the Bible showcases mankind's need for a deliverer and God's mission to provide. After the first created people—Adam and Eve—rebel against God and fall into sin, God promises a deliverer who will crush the head of the serpent who had deceived Eve.

Eve may have thought the son she bore was that deliverer (see Genesis 4:1), but the actual fulfillment looked much further into the future. Throughout the pages of the Old Testament God delivers His people over and over using men (and an occasional woman!) that He raises up, temporal saviors who point to someone greater to come.

Moses, who God raises up to deliver Israel from slavery in Egypt, bluntly tells this people to watch for and listen to the one God will send: *"The LORD your God will raise up for you a prophet like me from among you, from your countrymen, you shall listen to him"* (Deuteronomy 18:15). Remember, Moses was no ordinary prophet. God spoke to him face-to-face as one speaks to a friend (Exodus 33:11).

ONE STEP FURTHER:

Word Study: Deliver

Take some time this week to explore the Hebrew word translated "deliver" in Judges. Start by using an online concordance such as blueletterbible.org to identify how the word is used in Judges and elsewhere in the Bible. Note other ways the word is translated into English and see if you can figure out what biblical names stem from the same root! Record what you discover below.

Now in the Promised Land after 40 years of wandering in the wilderness after their deliverance from Egypt, the people once again find themselves in need of deliverers *over and over again,* but none—as we will see—is able to provide ultimate deliverance . . . yet!

Before we jump into Judges, let's look at Joshua 24 for some near context.

OBSERVE the TEXT of SCRIPTURE

Some of the people Joshua addresses in these verses had witnessed the Exodus as children and had seen for themselves the mighty acts of God throughout their lifetimes.

As you read Joshua 24:1-13, note how it sets the stage by reviewing God's work for and through the nation of Israel beginning with the call of Abraham. Let's let the text speak for itself.

READ Joshua 24:1-13 and **MARK** every reference to the *fathers.*

Joshua 24:1-13

1 *Then Joshua gathered all the tribes of Israel to Shechem, and called for the elders of Israel and for their heads and their judges and their officers; and they presented themselves before God.*

2 *Joshua said to all the people, "Thus says the LORD, the God of Israel, 'From ancient times your fathers lived beyond the River, namely, Terah, the father of Abraham and the father of Nahor, and they served other gods.*

3 *'Then I took your father Abraham from beyond the River, and led him through all the land of Canaan, and multiplied his descendants and gave him Isaac.*

4 *'To Isaac I gave Jacob and Esau, and to Esau I gave Mount Seir to possess it; but Jacob and his sons went down to Egypt.*

5 *'Then I sent Moses and Aaron, and I plagued Egypt by what I did in its midst; and afterward I brought you out.*

6 *'I brought your fathers out of Egypt, and you came to the sea; and Egypt pursued your fathers with chariots and horsemen to the Red Sea.*

7 *'But when they cried out to the LORD, He put darkness between you and the Egyptians, and brought the sea upon them and covered them; and your own eyes saw what I did in Egypt. And you lived in the wilderness for a long time.*

8 'Then I brought you into the land of the Amorites who lived beyond the Jordan, and they fought with you; and I gave them into your hand, and you took possession of their land when I destroyed them before you.

9 'Then Balak the son of Zippor, king of Moab, arose and fought against Israel, and he sent and summoned Balaam the son of Beor to curse you.

10 'But I was not willing to listen to Balaam. So he had to bless you, and I delivered you from his hand.

11 'You crossed the Jordan and came to Jericho; and the citizens of Jericho fought against you, and the Amorite and the Perizzite and the Canaanite and the Hittite and the Girgashite, the Hivite and the Jebusite. Thus I gave them into your hand.

12 'Then I sent the hornet before you and it drove out the two kings of the Amorites from before you, but not by your sword or your bow.

13 'I gave you a land on which you had not labored, and cities which you had not built, and you have lived in them; you are eating of vineyards and olive groves which you did not plant.'

DISCUSS with your GROUP or PONDER on your own . . .

Who does Joshua gather to Shechem and for what purpose?

Who is the main speaker in verses 2-13? Whose message is being delivered?

Where did Israel's "fathers" come from? What kind of people were they?

Do you think the "fathers" should have had knowledge of the One true God? Why/why not? Explain.

Who were the main characters mentioned in Israel's history and what are they known for?

Think for a moment about how familiar or unfamiliar you are with people and events from your parents' and grandparents' generations. Can you understand how easy it is for knowledge to stall between generations? Explain.

INDUCTIVE FOCUS:

Application—The Difference Between What Stands and Falls

As we study God's Word we can't stop at knowing what it says and what it means . . . we need to act on what we know! Jesus tells us plainly in Matthew 7:24-27 the difference that application makes:

"Therefore everyone who hears these words of Mine and acts on them, may be compared to a wise man who built his house on the rock. And the rain fell, and the floods came, and the winds blew and slammed against that house; and yet it did not fall, for it had been founded on the rock. Everyone who hears these words of Mine and does not act on them, will be like a foolish man who built his house on the sand. The rain fell, and the floods came, and the winds blew and slammed against that house; and it fell—and great was its fall."

If you are not an eyewitness to an event, what do you need in order to know history?

How are you doing at listening to the generation that came before you? How about at passing information on to the generation that is coming after you?

What truths about God do your kids, nieces, nephews, and other younger people in your life need to know? How can you help equip them to know God?

How *are you* doing at this?

What had the Exodus generation learned firsthand about God?

How had God responded to their cries for help?

How did He act on Israel's behalf? Who were some of the enemies God defeated?

What did God give the people of Israel? Why?

INDUCTIVE FOCUS:

Asking Questions of Everything!

One of the most effective ways to understand the Bible is to read slowly and carefully and then ask the basic investigative questions: *Who? What? When? Where? Why?* and *How?* The hardest part of Bible study for most people today is simply slowing down. Remember: Bible study is not a race!

OBSERVE the TEXT of SCRIPTURE

Let's move on to the second half of Joshua 24.

READ Joshua 24:14-33 and **MARK** every occurrence of *serve(d)*.

Joshua 24:14-33

14 "Now, therefore, fear the LORD and serve Him in sincerity and truth; and put away the gods which your fathers served beyond the River and in Egypt, and serve the LORD.

15 *"If it is disagreeable in your sight to serve the LORD, choose for yourselves today whom you will serve: whether the gods which your fathers served which were beyond the River, or the gods of the Amorites in whose land you are living; but as for me and my house, we will serve the LORD."*

16 *The people answered and said, "Far be it from us that we should forsake the LORD to serve other gods;*

17 *for the LORD our God is He who brought us and our fathers up out of the land of Egypt, from the house of bondage, and who did these great signs in our sight and preserved us through all the way in which we went and among all the peoples through whose midst we passed.*

18 *"The LORD drove out from before us all the peoples, even the Amorites who lived in the land. We also will serve the LORD, for He is our God."*

19 *Then Joshua said to the people, "You will not be able to serve the LORD, for He is a holy God. He is a jealous God; He will not forgive your transgression or your sins.*

20 *"If you forsake the LORD and serve foreign gods, then He will turn and do you harm and consume you after He has done good to you."*

21 *The people said to Joshua, "No, but we will serve the LORD."*

22 *Joshua said to the people, "You are witnesses against yourselves that you have chosen for yourselves the LORD, to serve Him." And they said, "We are witnesses."*

23 *"Now therefore, put away the foreign gods which are in your midst, and incline your hearts to the LORD, the God of Israel."*

24 *The people said to Joshua, "We will serve the LORD our God and we will obey His voice."*

25 *So Joshua made a covenant with the people that day, and made for them a statute and an ordinance in Shechem.*

26 *And Joshua wrote these words in the book of the law of God; and he took a large stone and set it up there under the oak that was by the sanctuary of the LORD.*

27 Joshua said to all the people, "Behold, this stone shall be for a witness against us, for it has heard all the words of the LORD which He spoke to us; thus it shall be for a witness against you, so that you do not deny your God."

28 Then Joshua dismissed the people, each to his inheritance.

29 It came about after these things that Joshua the son of Nun, the servant of the LORD, died, being one hundred and ten years old.

30 And they buried him in the territory of his inheritance in Timnath-serah, which is in the hill country of Ephraim, on the north of Mount Gaash.

31 Israel served the LORD all the days of Joshua and all the days of the elders who survived Joshua, and had known all the deeds of the LORD which He had done for Israel.

32 Now they buried the bones of Joseph, which the sons of Israel brought up from Egypt, at Shechem, in the piece of ground which Jacob had bought from the sons of Hamor the father of Shechem for one hundred pieces of money; and they became the inheritance of Joseph's sons.

33 And Eleazar the son of Aaron died; and they buried him at Gibeah of Phinehas his son, which was given him in the hill country of Ephraim.

DISCUSS with your GROUP or PONDER on your own . . .

What does Joshua shift his message to in verse 14?

What choice do the people face? What should be their reasonable response? Why?

What similar choices do you face? How does your life reflect who you serve?

What do the people covenant to do? How do they do and for how long? Why?

While the people pledge "We will serve the LORD" (v. 21) against Joshua's "You will not be able to serve the LORD, for He is a holy God," (v. 19), the book of Judges records Israel's downfall after Joshua and the elders who survive him die.

Victory characterizes the book of Joshua, but together we'll witness ongoing defeat during the entire period of the Judges.

@THE END OF THE DAY . . .

Take a few minutes to jot down your biggest application point from this week of study as well as your biggest remaining questions so far.

EXTRA

As we study the Bible together inductively, we'll always be observing, interpreting, and applying the text because these key components help us to accurately handle the Word of Truth. Using this basic approach, though, doesn't mean we all have to learn in the exact same way. We can use different tools and practices to help us learn and remember the timeless truths of God's Word.

Memorizing is a great tool for me because it causes me to see more closely how a writer is framing an argument. When I'm focusing on recall, I'm more apt to see repeated words and patterns—it's just how my brain works!

You may recall a text best by making a simple outline of it . . . or sketching what you saw in it. If you have extra time this week, do what you need to so that you'll remember the basic content of Lesson 1. Here are some ideas:

Memorize Key Verses

Hebrews 11:6

> *And without faith it is impossible to please Him, for he who comes to God must believe that He is and that He is a rewarder of those who seek Him.*

Joshua 24:23-24

> *"Now therefore, put away the foreign gods which are in your midst, and incline your hearts to the LORD, the God of Israel."*

> *The people said to Joshua, "We will serve the LORD our God and we will obey His voice."*

Joshua 24:31

> *Israel served the LORD all the days of Joshua and all the days of the elders who survived Joshua, and had known all the deeds of the LORD which He had done for Israel.*

Got another one? Write it down!

Create a Simple Outline

Hebrews 11 talks about . . .

Joshua 24:1-13 talks about . . .

Joshua 24:14-33 talks about . . .

"Tweet" It

Brevity can make us think more accurately. See if you can summarize the message of Joshua 24 in 140 characters or less.

#Hashtag It

Write a hashtag for Hebrews 11.

#

Write a hashtag for Joshua 24.

#

Sketch It

More of a visual learner? Use the space below to sketch out your takeaway points from Hebrews 11 and/or Joshua 24.

If you're thinking about memorizing any verses or passages, check out **www.Biblememory.com** (formerly Scripturetyper.com). I highly recommend this software that helps you memorize and keeps you honest by testing you on an ongoing basis!

The Peril of Not Knowing Your God

. . . and there arose another generation after them who did not know the LORD, nor yet the work which He had done for Israel.
—Judges 2:10b

Sin causes collateral damage. We don't like that thought. We ignore it, we dismiss it, and we often try to wish it away, but the truth remains. Your sin, my sin, affects more than the sinner. Your sin's consequence doesn't stop with you, mine doesn't stop with me. My anger spills out, your unkind words draw blood, our impatience takes its toll on others in our world.

Compromise with sin is deadly. Sin clogs up ears, stiffens necks, and hardens hearts. When sin rules a generation, when truth stumbles in the streets, entire cultures shift.

As we'll see in the book of Judges, when one generation compromised with sin, the next generation did not even know the LORD.

REMEMBERING

Take a few minutes to summarize what you learned last week.

OBSERVE the TEXT of SCRIPTURE

This week we'll look at Judges 1 and 2. While the text is included in the lesson, feel free to use your own Bible if you prefer. Because the chapter breaks in the English translation of the Bible don't follow the natural flow of the text, we'll look at Judges 1 through Judges 2:5 as one segment and then study Judges 2 as a separate unit starting at verse 6.

READ Judges 1–Judges 2:5 and **MARK** every reference to the phrases *did not drive out* and *lived among*. Also **MARK** every reference to *the LORD/ God*.

Judges 1:1–2:5

1   *Now it came about after the death of Joshua that the sons of Israel inquired of the LORD, saying, "Who shall go up first for us against the Canaanites, to fight against them?"*

2   *The LORD said, "Judah shall go up; behold, I have given the land into his hand."*

3   *Then Judah said to Simeon his brother, "Come up with me into the territory allotted me, that we may fight against the Canaanites; and I in turn will go with you into the territory allotted you." So Simeon went with him.*

4   *Judah went up, and the LORD gave the Canaanites and the Perizzites into their hands, and they defeated ten thousand men at Bezek.*

5   *They found Adoni-bezek in Bezek and fought against him, and they defeated the Canaanites and the Perizzites.*

6   *But Adoni-bezek fled; and they pursued him and caught him and cut off his thumbs and big toes.*

7   Adoni-bezek said, "Seventy kings with their thumbs and their big toes cut off used to gather up scraps under my table; as I have done, so God has repaid me." So they brought him to Jerusalem and he died there.

8   Then the sons of Judah fought against Jerusalem and captured it and struck it with the edge of the sword and set the city on fire.

9   Afterward the sons of Judah went down to fight against the Canaanites living in the hill country and in the Negev and in the lowland.

10 So Judah went against the Canaanites who lived in Hebron (now the name of Hebron formerly was Kiriath-arba); and they struck Sheshai and Ahiman and Talmai.

11 Then from there he went against the inhabitants of Debir (now the name of Debir formerly was Kiriath-sepher).

12 And Caleb said, "The one who attacks Kiriath-sepher and captures it, I will even give him my daughter Achsah for a wife."

13 Othniel the son of Kenaz, Caleb's younger brother, captured it; so he gave him his daughter Achsah for a wife.

14 Then it came about when she came to him, that she persuaded him to ask her father for a field. Then she alighted from her donkey, and Caleb said to her, "What do you want?"

15 She said to him, "Give me a blessing, since you have given me the land of the Negev, give me also springs of water." So Caleb gave her the upper springs and the lower springs.

16 The descendants of the Kenite, Moses' father-in-law, went up from the city of palms with the sons of Judah, to the wilderness of Judah which is in the south of Arad; and they went and lived with the people.

17 Then Judah went with Simeon his brother, and they struck the Canaanites living in Zephath, and utterly destroyed it. So the name of the city was called Hormah.

18 And Judah took Gaza with its territory and Ashkelon with its territory and Ekron with its territory.

19 Now the LORD was with Judah, and they took possession of the hill country; but they could not drive out the inhabitants of the valley because they had iron chariots.

20 Then they gave Hebron to Caleb, as Moses had promised; and he drove out from there the three sons of Anak.

21 But the sons of Benjamin did not drive out the Jebusites who lived in Jerusalem; so the Jebusites have lived with the sons of Benjamin in Jerusalem to this day.

22 Likewise the house of Joseph went up against Bethel, and the LORD was with them.

23 The house of Joseph spied out Bethel (now the name of the city was formerly Luz).

24 The spies saw a man coming out of the city and they said to him, "Please show us the entrance to the city and we will treat you kindly."

25 So he showed them the entrance to the city, and they struck the city with the edge of the sword, but they let the man and all his family go free.

26 The man went into the land of the Hittites and built a city and named it Luz which is its name to this day.

27 But Manasseh did not take possession of Beth-shean and its villages, or Taanach and its villages, or the inhabitants of Dor and its villages, or the inhabitants of Ibleam and its villages, or the inhabitants of Megiddo and its villages; so the Canaanites persisted in living in that land.

28 It came about when Israel became strong, that they put the Canaanites to forced labor, but they did not drive them out completely.

29 Ephraim did not drive out the Canaanites who were living in Gezer; so the Canaanites lived in Gezer among them.

30 Zebulun did not drive out the inhabitants of Kitron, or the inhabitants of Nahalol; so the Canaanites lived among them and became subject to forced labor.

31 Asher did not drive out the inhabitants of Acco, or the inhabitants of Sidon, or of Ahlab, or of Achzib, or of Helbah, or of Aphik, or of Rehob.

32 So the Asherites lived among the Canaanites, the inhabitants of the land; for they did not drive them out.

33 Naphtali did not drive out the inhabitants of Beth-shemesh, or the inhabitants of Beth-anath, but lived among the Canaanites, the inhabitants of the land; and the inhabitants of Beth-shemesh and Beth-anath became forced labor for them.

34 Then the Amorites forced the sons of Dan into the hill country, for they did not allow them to come down to the valley;

35 yet the Amorites persisted in living in Mount Heres, in Aijalon and in Shaalbim; but when the power of the house of Joseph grew strong, they became forced labor.

36 The border of the Amorites ran from the ascent of Akrabbim, from Sela and upward.

2:1 Now the angel of the LORD came up from Gilgal to Bochim. And he said, "I brought you up out of Egypt and led you into the land which I have sworn to your fathers; and I said, 'I will never break My covenant with you,

2 and as for you, you shall make no covenant with the inhabitants of this land; you shall tear down their altars.' But you have not obeyed Me; what is this you have done?

3 "Therefore I also said, 'I will not drive them out before you; but they will become as thorns in your sides and their gods will be a snare to you.' "

4 When the angel of the LORD spoke these words to all the sons of Israel, the people lifted up their voices and wept.

5 So they named that place Bochim; and there they sacrificed to the LORD.

FYI:

Tribes Not Individuals

When the text refers to "Judah" and "Simeon" at the beginning of the Judges 1, it almost sounds like God is talking to individual people, especially when we read about Judah talking to his brother Simeon in 1:3. The "original" Judah and Simeon, both sons of Jacob, were long dead by the time of the judges. When we read their names in Judges, it refers to the tribes that bear their names. The same holds true for Benjamin, Asher, Manasseh, and the rest.

The City of Palms

Deuteronomy 34:3 refers to Jericho as "the city of palm trees." This was the first city that Israel attacked and conquered when God brought His people into the Promised Land under Joshua's leadership.

DISCUSS with your GROUP or PONDER on your own . . .

What event initiates the period of the judges of Israel?

How well do the people of Israel start out in Judges 1? How would you describe their relationship with God? What from the text makes you think this?

What do the people ask God? What does He tell them to do? How does He assure them?

How does the tribe of Judah respond to God's instruction? Do they obey God in *all* specifics? Do they *ad lib* at all? If so, where?

Who does Judah go up to fight against in verses 3-10? Note both the people and the cities involved. What happens in each instance?

Where do we have the clear Word of God today? How are you doing at following God's revealed Word?

Who is introduced in verses 11-15? What do they do and what results?

What difficulty does Judah encounter in verse 19? What potential problem does this set up?

How does the remainder of Judges 1 describe and evaluate the other tribes' encounters with the land's inhabitants? What phrases summarize their behavior and subsequent condition?

ONE STEP FURTHER:

Word Study: Chariots

If you have some time this week, use a concordance to see where chariots have appeared in the Bible up to this point. *Who had chariots? What were they used for? What happened to the chariots?* When you've found the answers, respond to this question: *Should chariots have been a concern for the children of Israel? Why/why not?*

DIGGING DEEPER
Caleb and Joshua: The Backstory

Want to know more about Caleb and Joshua? Why not invest some time this week learning about them while honing your inductive Bible study skills?!

Use a concordance to locate where each shows up in the Bible and treat yourself to some independent study. Record what you learn about each man and, as we study, consider how the judges compare with these two godly leaders of Israel.

Caleb:

Joshua:

For an online concordance, one of my favorites is www.blueletterbible.org.

Do you ever find yourself living with sin because, for whatever reason, you've not driven it out from your life? If so, how is that going for you? Is there something you know you need to change? If so, write it down and ask God to empower you to follow Him in your next steps.

Who appears in Judges 2:1-3? What message does he bring to the people?

How had God shown His faithfulness to the people of Israel in the past?

What were the Israelites supposed to do when they came into the land? Why? Had God been clear about this? What did they do instead?

What consequence will they now face? How do the people respond to the news?

ONE STEP FURTHER:

Gilgal
If you have some extra time this week, use a concordance to search on "Gilgal." Find out what significant event was commemorated there and record your findings below. As you do, consider how this event should have continued to shape the people's faith.

OBSERVE the TEXT of SCRIPTURE

While Judges 1 presents a basic narrative of what the tribes did and did not do, Judges 2 gives a more theological perspective on their behavior.

READ Judges 2:6-23. CIRCLE references to *the sons of Israel* including pronouns and UNDERLINE all the verbs associated with them that show what they did or did not do. Then read the passage again and MARK all of the references to *the LORD* and all references to the *judges*.

Judges 2:6-23

6   When Joshua had dismissed the people, the sons of Israel went each to his inheritance to possess the land.

7   The people served the LORD all the days of Joshua, and all the days of the elders who survived Joshua, who had seen all the great work of the LORD which He had done for Israel.

8   Then Joshua the son of Nun, the servant of the LORD, died at the age of one hundred and ten.

9   And they buried him in the territory of his inheritance in Timnath-heres, in the hill country of Ephraim, north of Mount Gaash.

10 All that generation also were gathered to their fathers; and there arose another generation after them who did not know the LORD, nor yet the work which He had done for Israel.

11 Then the sons of Israel did evil in the sight of the LORD and served the Baals,

12 and they forsook the LORD, the God of their fathers, who had brought them out of the land of Egypt, and followed other gods from among the gods of the peoples who were around them, and bowed themselves down to them; thus they provoked the LORD to anger.

13 So they forsook the LORD and served Baal and the Ashtaroth.

14 The anger of the LORD burned against Israel, and He gave them into the hands of plunderers who plundered them; and He sold them into the hands of their enemies around them, so that they could no longer stand before their enemies.

15 Wherever they went, the hand of the LORD was against them for evil, as the LORD had spoken and as the LORD had sworn to them, so that they were severely distressed.

16 Then the LORD raised up judges who delivered them from the hands of those who plundered them.

17 Yet they did not listen to their judges, for they played the harlot after other gods and bowed themselves down to them. They turned aside quickly from the way in which their fathers had walked in obeying the commandments of the LORD; they did not do as their fathers.

18 When the LORD raised up judges for them, the LORD was with the judge and delivered them from the hand of their enemies all the days of the judge; for the LORD was moved to pity by their groaning because of those who oppressed and afflicted them.

19 But it came about when the judge died, that they would turn back and act more corruptly than their fathers, in following other gods to serve them and bow down to them; they did not abandon their practices or their stubborn ways.

20 So the anger of the LORD burned against Israel, and He said, "Because this nation has transgressed My covenant which I commanded their fathers and has not listened to My voice,

21 I also will no longer drive out before them any of the nations which Joshua left when he died,

22 in order to test Israel by them, whether they will keep the way of the LORD to walk in it as their fathers did, or not."

23 So the LORD allowed those nations to remain, not driving them out quickly; and He did not give them into the hand of Joshua.

DISCUSS with your GROUP or PONDER on your own . . .

What do we learn about Joshua in Judges 2:6-9?

How did the people act while Joshua and the elders who survived him were alive?

What happened to the next generation? Why?

Have you seen truth falter between generations? If so, explain what you've experienced.

Did the people literally not know facts about God after one generation or may this be describing a lack of *true* relationship? Explain your answer from the text and/or from other Scripture. (Keep this question in the front of your mind as we continue studying.)

Is there a difference between knowing about God and knowing God? Explain.

What happens when a generation or culture doesn't have a knowledge of God?

Look back at where you marked references to the "sons of Israel" and list how they lived after Joshua's death.

What does God do in response to their disobedience?

Who were the judges? List everything you learned about them from Judges 2.

What is God going to use the nations for in Israel's corporate life? Why?

Do you see a behavioral cycle in verses 11-23? See if you can identify it and draw it in the space below.

Ask God About Application

Don't stop with asking God to help you understand the text of Scripture. Ask Him to help you apply it, too! If you haven't considered how what you're learning will change the way you think and act, you haven't finished your Bible study!

What did you learn about God in Judges 2? Look at every place you marked a reference to Him and record what you learned.

Which of these truths do you think our culture most needs to learn about Him? Why?

What truth about God did *you* most need to learn or be reminded of today? Why? How can this affect your thinking and actions this week?

@THE END OF THE DAY . . .

As we move through Judges, we will continue to see Israel spiral in a downward cycle of sin. Israel sins, God sends a nation to oppress them, the people eventually cry out for help, and God raises up a deliverer to save them. When the judge dies, the people return to their sin and behave even worse than they had before, and the cycle begins again. With each deliverer, it will become more and more obvious that people—then and now—need far more than any human being can offer!

EXTRA
MEMORIZE | TWEET | POST | DRAW | HASHTAG | ENCODE | REMEMBER

Congratulations! You're done with your homework! This part really is for fun and to help you solidify what you've learned in the way that best works for you. Seriously, see what is helpful here and use it; what doesn't work for you . . . leave it!

Memorize a Key Verse for Each Chapter

Judges 1:2
> *The LORD said, "Judah shall go up; behold, I have given the land into his hand."*

Judges 2:10
> *All that generation also were gathered to their fathers; and there arose another generation after them who did not know the LORD, nor yet the work which He had done for Israel.*

Prefer a different one? Write it down . . .

"Tweet" It

Summarize the message of Judges 1 and 2 in 140 characters or less.

#Hashtag It

Write a hashtag for Judges 1.

\#

Write a hashtag for Judges 2.

\#

Map It!

Use your Internet skills to find a map of Israel during the time of the judges and sketch the locations you learn about here in your book. If you're artsy, draw what happens in the appropriate locations on the map!

How to do an Online Word Study

For use with www.blueletterbible.org

1. Type in the Bible verse. Change the version to NASB. Click the "Go" button.
2. When you arrive at the next screen, you will see a "Tools" button to the left of your verse.
   Hover your mouse over the "Tools" button and select "Interlinear" to bring up concordance information.
3. Click on the Strong's number that links to the original word in Greek or Hebrew.

Clicking this number will bring up another screen that will give you a brief definition of the word as well as a list of every occurrence of the Greek word in the New Testament or Hebrew word in the Old Testament. Before running to the dictionary definition, scan places where this word is used in Scripture and examine the contexts where it is used.

A Hopeful Beginning

They [the nations] were for testing Israel, to find out if they would obey the commandments of the LORD, which He had commanded their fathers through Moses.
—Judges 3:4

Throughout the later pages of Judges, a phrase repeats like a tragic chorus: "In those days there was no king in Israel; every man did what was right in his own eyes."

While defeat and sin cycles mark the entire era of the judges, we will see a descent, a downward spiral as we move through the book. The leaders we'll look at this week in Judges 3–5, however, stand at the top of the pack!

Not As Much As It Looks Like!
Remember, I've included the Scripture text in the workbook so the assignment is shorter than it appears! Seriously!!

REMEMBERING

Take a few minutes to summarize what you learned last week.

OBSERVE the TEXT of SCRIPTURE

In Judges 3 we meet the first three judges: Othniel, Ehud, and Shamgar.

READ Judges 3. **MARK** references to *the LORD*, to *the sons of Israel* (including pronouns), and to the judges (*Othniel, Ehud,* and *Shamgar*).

Judges 3

1 *Now these are the nations which the LORD left, to test Israel by them (that is, all who had not experienced any of the wars of Canaan;*

2 *only in order that the generations of the sons of Israel might be taught war, those who had not experienced it formerly).*

3 These nations are: *the five lords of the Philistines and all the Canaanites and the Sidonians and the Hivites who lived in Mount Lebanon, from Mount Baal-hermon as far as Lebo-hamath.*

4 *They were for testing Israel, to find out if they would obey the commandments of the LORD, which He had commanded their fathers through Moses.*

5 *The sons of Israel lived among the Canaanites, the Hittites, the Amorites, the Perizzites, the Hivites, and the Jebusites;*

6 *and they took their daughters for themselves as wives, and gave their own daughters to their sons, and served their gods.*

7 *The sons of Israel did what was evil in the sight of the LORD, and forgot the LORD their God and served the Baals and the Asheroth.*

8 *Then the anger of the LORD was kindled against Israel, so that He sold them into the hands of Cushan-rishathaim king of Mesopotamia; and the sons of Israel served Cushan-rishathaim eight years.*

9 When the sons of Israel cried to the LORD, the LORD raised up a deliverer for the sons of Israel to deliver them, Othniel the son of Kenaz, Caleb's younger brother.

10 The Spirit of the LORD came upon him, and he judged Israel. When he went out to war, the LORD gave Cushan-rishathaim king of Mesopotamia into his hand, so that he prevailed over Cushan-rishathaim.

11 Then the land had rest forty years. And Othniel the son of Kenaz died.

12 Now the sons of Israel again did evil in the sight of the LORD. So the LORD strengthened Eglon the king of Moab against Israel, because they had done evil in the sight of the LORD.

13 And he gathered to himself the sons of Ammon and Amalek; and he went and defeated Israel, and they possessed the city of the palm trees.

14 The sons of Israel served Eglon the king of Moab eighteen years.

15 But when the sons of Israel cried to the LORD, the LORD raised up a deliverer for them, Ehud the son of Gera, the Benjamite, a left-handed man. And the sons of Israel sent tribute by him to Eglon the king of Moab.

16 Ehud made himself a sword which had two edges, a cubit in length, and he bound it on his right thigh under his cloak.

17 He presented the tribute to Eglon king of Moab. Now Eglon was a very fat man.

18 It came about when he had finished presenting the tribute, that he sent away the people who had carried the tribute.

19 But he himself turned back from the idols which were at Gilgal, and said, "I have a secret message for you, O king." And he said, "Keep silence." And all who attended him left him.

20 Ehud came to him while he was sitting alone in his cool roof chamber. And Ehud said, "I have a message from God for you." And he arose from his seat.

21 Ehud stretched out his left hand, took the sword from his right thigh and thrust it into his belly.

22 The handle also went in after the blade, and the fat closed over the blade, for he did not draw the sword out of his belly; and the refuse came out.

23 *Then Ehud went out into the vestibule and shut the doors of the roof chamber behind him, and locked them.*

24 *When he had gone out, his servants came and looked, and behold, the doors of the roof chamber were locked; and they said, "He is only relieving himself in the cool room."*

25 *They waited until they became anxious; but behold, he did not open the doors of the roof chamber. Therefore they took the key and opened them, and behold, their master had fallen to the floor dead.*

26 *Now Ehud escaped while they were delaying, and he passed by the idols and escaped to Seirah.*

27 *It came about when he had arrived, that he blew the trumpet in the hill country of Ephraim; and the sons of Israel went down with him from the hill country, and he was in front of them.*

28 *He said to them, "Pursue them, for the LORD has given your enemies the Moabites into your hands." So they went down after him and seized the fords of the Jordan opposite Moab, and did not allow anyone to cross.*

29 *They struck down at that time about ten thousand Moabites, all robust and valiant men; and no one escaped.*

30 *So Moab was subdued that day under the hand of Israel. And the land was undisturbed for eighty years.*

31 *After him came Shamgar the son of Anath, who struck down six hundred Philistines with an oxgoad; and he also saved Israel.*

DISCUSS with your GROUP or PONDER on your own . . .

What is Israel's cultural and spiritual condition at the beginning of Judges 3?

How is God now going to use the nations that Israel did not drive out?

In what ways are the Israelites bonding to the inhabitants of the land? How are we tempted to do similar things today?

What happens when Israel does evil in the sight of the LORD?

What specific nations oppress Israel and for how long? Who does God use to deliver them? (Use the chart below for simple reference.)

Oppressor	Duration	Deliverer	Land Rests

How does God respond when His oppressed people cry out to Him?

Who is the first judge recorded in this chapter? Describe him. Who is he related to? What does he do?

What happens when he dies?

Why were Israel's enemies able to defeat and oppress her?

How does sin weaken nations and people?

Who does God raise up as a judge to deliver His people from Moab? Describe him.

FYI:

Moab and Israel

Unlike some of Israel's surrounding nations and oppressors, the Moabites were distant relatives. When Abraham followed God's call to the land of Canaan, he traveled with his wife Sarah and his nephew Lot. One of Lot's sons was—you guessed it!—Moab! Moab's land was in the Transjordan region to the east of Canaan.

ONE STEP FURTHER:

Also, During the Time of the Judges . . .

If you have some extra time this week, see if you can figure out what other book of the Bible contains events that took place during this same period in biblical history. Then note the touchpoints it has with the account of Ehud. Record your findings below.

Who is Eglon? Where is he from?

Where does the encounter between Ehud and Eglon take place? What is significant about this? (If you're not sure, check out Joshua 4.)

How does Ehud deliver Israel? How do the people help?

How long does the land remain undisturbed?

Shamgar the Tribeless

Othniel was from Judah, Ehud from Benjamin, but Judges attributes no tribe to Shamgar. Shamgar's name suggests he was a non-Israelite God used to deliver His people.

Who is the final person mentioned in Judges 3? What does he do?

OBSERVE the TEXT of SCRIPTURE

Judges 4 presents a specific account of Deborah and Barak while Judges 5 gives a poetic summary of the same event.

READ Judges 4. **MARK** distinctively references to the major characters: *Jabin, Sisera, Deborah, Barak,* and *Jael*.

Judges 4

1   *Then the sons of Israel again did evil in the sight of the LORD, after Ehud died.*

2   *And the LORD sold them into the hand of Jabin king of Canaan, who reigned in Hazor; and the commander of his army was Sisera, who lived in Harosheth-hagoyim.*

3   *The sons of Israel cried to the LORD; for he had nine hundred iron chariots, and he oppressed the sons of Israel severely for twenty years.*

4   *Now Deborah, a prophetess, the wife of Lappidoth, was judging Israel at that time.*

5   *She used to sit under the palm tree of Deborah between Ramah and Bethel in the hill country of Ephraim; and the sons of Israel came up to her for judgment.*

6   *Now she sent and summoned Barak the son of Abinoam from Kedesh-naphtali, and said to him, "Behold, the LORD, the God of Israel, has commanded, 'Go and march to Mount Tabor, and take with you ten thousand men from the sons of Naphtali and from the sons of Zebulun.*

7 'I will draw out to you Sisera, the commander of Jabin's army, with his chariots and his many troops to the river Kishon, and I will give him into your hand.' "

8 Then Barak said to her, "If you will go with me, then I will go; but if you will not go with me, I will not go."

9 She said, "I will surely go with you; nevertheless, the honor shall not be yours on the journey that you are about to take, for the LORD will sell Sisera into the hands of a woman." Then Deborah arose and went with Barak to Kedesh.

10 Barak called Zebulun and Naphtali together to Kedesh, and ten thousand men went up with him; Deborah also went up with him.

11 Now Heber the Kenite had separated himself from the Kenites, from the sons of Hobab the father-in-law of Moses, and had pitched his tent as far away as the oak in Zaanannim, which is near Kedesh.

12 Then they told Sisera that Barak the son of Abinoam had gone up to Mount Tabor.

13 Sisera called together all his chariots, nine hundred iron chariots, and all the people who were with him, from Harosheth-hagoyim to the river Kishon.

14 Deborah said to Barak, "Arise! For this is the day in which the LORD has given Sisera into your hands; behold, the LORD has gone out before you." So Barak went down from Mount Tabor with ten thousand men following him.

15 The LORD routed Sisera and all his chariots and all his army with the edge of the sword before Barak; and Sisera alighted from his chariot and fled away on foot.

16 But Barak pursued the chariots and the army as far as Harosheth-hagoyim, and all the army of Sisera fell by the edge of the sword; not even one was left.

17 Now Sisera fled away on foot to the tent of Jael the wife of Heber the Kenite, for there was peace between Jabin the king of Hazor and the house of Heber the Kenite.

18 Jael went out to meet Sisera, and said to him, "Turn aside, my master, turn aside to me! Do not be afraid." And he turned aside to her into the tent, and she covered him with a rug.

19 He said to her, "Please give me a little water to drink, for I am
    thirsty." So she opened a bottle of milk and gave him a drink; then
    she covered him.

20 He said to her, "Stand in the doorway of the tent, and it shall be if
    anyone comes and inquires of you, and says, 'Is there anyone here?'
    that you shall say, 'No.'"

21 But Jael, Heber's wife, took a tent peg and seized a hammer in her
    hand, and went secretly to him and drove the peg into his temple,
    and it went through into the ground; for he was sound asleep and
    exhausted. So he died.

22 And behold, as Barak pursued Sisera, Jael came out to meet him
    and said to him, "Come, and I will show you the man whom you
    are seeking." And he entered with her, and behold Sisera was lying
    dead with the tent peg in his temple.

23 So God subdued on that day Jabin the king of Canaan before the
    sons of Israel.

24 The hand of the sons of Israel pressed heavier and heavier upon
    Jabin the king of Canaan, until they had destroyed Jabin the king of
    Canaan.

DISCUSS with your GROUP or PONDER on your own . . .

What predicament is Israel in at the beginning of Judges 4? How long had
they been in this situation and why?

What foreign power is oppressing them? What key advantage does the
enemy have? Where have you seen this previously in Judges?

What are some modern comparisons? What "iron chariots" do we face today?

Who is judging Israel in Judges 4? Describe her from the text. (What does she do, where does she live, etc.?)

ONE STEP FURTHER:

Women of Stature

Deborah stands out on the Judges' landscape not only because she is an upright leader during crooked times but also because she is a woman. If you have some extra time this week compare Deborah and Jael—the unlikely heroine of the story—both women used mightily of God to save Israel but each working in different spheres of influence. Record below what you learn and how you will apply it.

What message does Deborah bring to Barak and how does he respond? Describe him from the text.

What do you think of Barak's response? Do you relate to him? Are you annoyed by his response? Explain your answer.

Do you ever respond based on what you see around you as opposed to what God has told you in His Word? If so, how has that been working?

Describe the battle. Who are the main combatants? How many are there? What happens?

Who does the text credit for giving the army the victory?

What happens after Sisera flees on foot?

Who is Jael and what does she do?

What nationality is Jael? Does she have any reason to involve herself in the conflict? Who does she side with?

How does God use Deborah? How does God use Jael?

How is God using you?

Does fear ever stop you from going where God has called you to go or doing what He has called you to do? Explain. How can truths that you've learned about God in this account help you to respond differently?

OBSERVE the TEXT of SCRIPTURE

Judges 4 narrated the basics of Israel's defeat of Sisera and Canaan. The Song of Deborah and Barak in Judges 5 recaps the events of Judges 4 in poetic form and gives more insight into God's role in Sisera's defeat.

Note: *Due to the poetic form, you will notice capitalizations in the middle of sentences. These represent line breaks in the NASB text.*

READ Judges 5. **MARK** references to water, weather or natural disasters. Also **MARK** references to *the LORD*, *Deborah*, *Jael*, and *Sisera*.

Judges 5

1   Then Deborah and Barak the son of Abinoam sang on that day, saying,

2   "That the leaders led in Israel, That the people volunteered, Bless the LORD!

3   "Hear, O kings; give ear, O rulers! I—to the LORD, I will sing, I will sing praise to the LORD, the God of Israel.

4   "LORD, when You went out from Seir, When You marched from the field of Edom, The earth quaked, the heavens also dripped, Even the clouds dripped water.

5   "The mountains quaked at the presence of the LORD, This Sinai, at the presence of the LORD, the God of Israel.

6   "In the days of Shamgar the son of Anath, In the days of Jael, the highways were deserted, And travelers went by roundabout ways.

7   "The peasantry ceased, they ceased in Israel, Until I, Deborah, arose, Until I arose, a mother in Israel.

8   "New gods were chosen; Then war was in the gates. Not a shield or a spear was seen Among forty thousand in Israel.

9   "My heart goes out to the commanders of Israel, The volunteers among the people; Bless the LORD!

10   "You who ride on white donkeys, You who sit on rich carpets, And you who travel on the road—sing!

11   "At the sound of those who divide flocks among the watering places, There they shall recount the righteous deeds of the LORD, The righteous deeds for His peasantry in Israel. Then the people of the LORD went down to the gates.

12   "Awake, awake, Deborah; Awake, awake, sing a song! Arise, Barak, and take away your captives, O son of Abinoam.

13   "Then survivors came down to the nobles; The people of the LORD came down to me as warriors.

14 *"From Ephraim those whose root is in Amalek came down,
Following you, Benjamin, with your peoples; From Machir
commanders came down, And from Zebulun those who wield the
staff of office.*

15 *"And the princes of Issachar were with Deborah; As was Issachar,
so was Barak; Into the valley they rushed at his heels; Among the
divisions of Reuben There were great resolves of heart.*

16 *"Why did you sit among the sheepfolds, To hear the piping for the
flocks? Among the divisions of Reuben There were great searchings
of heart.*

17 *"Gilead remained across the Jordan; And why did Dan stay in ships?
Asher sat at the seashore, And remained by its landings.*

18 *"Zebulun was a people who despised their lives even to death, And
Naphtali also, on the high places of the field.*

19 *"The kings came and fought; Then fought the kings of Canaan At
Taanach near the waters of Megiddo; They took no plunder in silver.*

20 *"The stars fought from heaven, From their courses they fought
against Sisera.*

21 *"The torrent of Kishon swept them away, The ancient torrent, the
torrent Kishon. O my soul, march on with strength.*

22 *"Then the horses' hoofs beat From the dashing, the dashing of his
valiant steeds.*

23 *'Curse Meroz,' said the angel of the LORD, 'Utterly curse its
inhabitants; Because they did not come to the help of the LORD, To
the help of the LORD against the warriors.'*

24 *"Most blessed of women is Jael, The wife of Heber the Kenite; Most
blessed is she of women in the tent.*

25 *"He asked for water and she gave him milk; In a magnificent bowl
she brought him curds.*

26 *"She reached out her hand for the tent peg, And her right hand for
the workmen's hammer. Then she struck Sisera, she smashed his
head; And she shattered and pierced his temple.*

27 *"Between her feet he bowed, he fell, he lay; Between her feet he
bowed, he fell; Where he bowed, there he fell dead.*

28 *"Out of the window she looked and lamented, The mother of Sisera through the lattice, 'Why does his chariot delay in coming? Why do the hoofbeats of his chariots tarry?'*

29 *"Her wise princesses would answer her, Indeed she repeats her words to herself,*

30 *'Are they not finding, are they not dividing the spoil? A maiden, two maidens for every warrior; To Sisera a spoil of dyed work, A spoil of dyed work embroidered, Dyed work of double embroidery on the neck of the spoiler?'*

31 *"Thus let all Your enemies perish, O LORD; But let those who love Him be like the rising of the sun in its might." And the land was undisturbed for forty years.*

DISCUSS with your GROUP or PONDER on your own . . .

What were the days like before the battle?

What effect had the severe oppression had on the people?

Do you see any parallels with today? Cultural ones? Responses in people? Explain.

According to Judges 5:8, how did Israel wind up in this situation in the first place? Do we do the same things today? Explain.

How did the people change according to Judges 5:2?

What difference does a godly leader make?

What difference do committed followers or volunteers make?

Of those two categories, which do you relate to most often? Explain. What can you learn from this account that you can apply in your role as either a leader or volunteer?

Look back to where you marked references to water, weather, earthquakes and such. Jot down what happened. Pay close attention to verses 4-5 and 19-22.

Now, in your own words, summarize what the weather was like on the day of battle. What happened to the river? How did it affect Sisera's chariots?

Why do you think Sisera abandoned his chariot to take off on foot?

How did the different tribes respond to the battle? Which ones helped? What did others do?

According to verses 23-24 who is cursed? Who is blessed? Why?

How do Jael's actions compare with the behavior of the inhabitants of Meroz?

What women speak in verses 28-30? What do we learn from them about Canaanite war practices? What did they do with women of conquered countries?

According to verse 31, what undesirable category was Sisera a part of?

FYI:

Meroz the Cursed

Meroz was a town of Israel that came under a curse because they did not fight for the LORD. Today we can only speculate where the cursed city once stood since it was wiped off the face of the earth. This cursed Israelite city that essentially behaved like the Canaanites sits in stark contrast to Jael, the blessed Gentile woman, who stood with Israel and fought for the LORD against the Canaanite commander.

In the face of ungodliness today, is God calling you to be a godly
leader among His people or is He calling you to be a faithful follower or
volunteer? Explain.

How are you going to respond?

What difference does knowing that God is the ultimate leader, the ultimate
deliverer make when you're faced with fear either of rising up as a leader
or involving yourself as a volunteer and follower?

@THE END OF THE DAY . . .

Not everyone is called to lead, but all of Jesus' sheep are called to follow
Him, the one true Deliverer! Like it or not, sometimes following Him
involves leading others. This week, ask God if you are following Him well,
if you are where He wants you to be. If you've been called to follow others
and volunteer, are you following well? If you've been called to lead, are
you doing so with diligence?

EXTRA

MEMORIZE | TWEET | POST | DRAW | HASHTAG | ENCODE | REMEMBER

Remember, this part is for fun! No guilt if you don't have the time, the energy, or the inclination to even read it!

Memorize a Key Verse for Each Chapter

Judges 3:7

> *The sons of Israel did what was evil in the sight of the LORD, and forgot the LORD their God and served the Baals and the Asheroth.*

Judges 4:8-9

> *Then Barak said to her, "If you will go with me, then I will go; but if you will not go with me, I will not go."*
>
> *She said, "I will surely go with you; nevertheless, the honor shall not be yours on the journey that you are about to take, for the LORD will sell Sisera into the hands of a woman." Then Deborah arose and went with Barak to Kedesh.*

Judges 5:2

> *"That the leaders led in Israel,*
> *That the people volunteered,*
> *Bless the LORD!*

Prefer a different one? Write it down . . .

"Tweet" It

Summarize the message of Judges 3 in 140 characters or less.

Summarize the message of Judges 4 and 5 in 140 characters or less.

#Hashtag It

Write a #hashtag for Judges 3.

\#

Write a #hashtag for Judges 4.

\#

Write a #hashtag for Judges 5.

\#

Draw It!

Sketch simple drawings of this week's judges!

A "Valiant Warrior"

The LORD looked at him [Gideon] and said, "Go in this your strength and deliver Israel from the hand of Midian. Have I not sent you?"
—Judges 6:14

Confidence. When opposition rises and oppressors prevail, confidence often leaves the room. Gideon's certainly did during the time of the Midianite invasions. Fear ruled his heart until the LORD raised him up to be a "valiant warrior" through whom He would deliver His people.

As we walk with Gideon this week in Judges 6–8 and see him deal with emotions on life's mountains and its valleys, watch for changes in his confidence. When does fearful Gideon become confident and where does his confidence rest? Sorry in advance that it may hit a little close to home . . . I know it did for me!

REMEMBERING

Take a few minutes to review what you've learned so far in Judges.

What has been your main application so far? How is what you're learning changing the way you think and act?

OBSERVE the TEXT of SCRIPTURE

Judges 6–8 introduce us to Gideon. As you read these chapters, be sure to watch for the change in this man.

READ Judges 6:1-10 and **MARK** references to *Midian* and *the Midianties*. Be sure to include pronouns.

Judges 6:1-10

1 Then the sons of Israel did what was evil in the sight of the LORD; and the LORD gave them into the hands of Midian seven years.

2 The power of Midian prevailed against Israel. Because of Midian the sons of Israel made for themselves the dens which were in the mountains and the caves and the strongholds.

3 For it was when Israel had sown, that the Midianites would come up with the Amalekites and the sons of the east and go against them.

4 So they would camp against them and destroy the produce of the earth as far as Gaza, and leave no sustenance in Israel as well as no sheep, ox, or donkey.

5 For they would come up with their livestock and their tents, they would come in like locusts for number, both they and their camels were innumerable; and they came into the land to devastate it.

6 So Israel was brought very low because of Midian, and the sons of Israel cried to the LORD.

7 Now it came about when the sons of Israel cried to the LORD on account of Midian,

8 that the LORD sent a prophet to the sons of Israel, and he said to them, "Thus says the LORD, the God of Israel, 'It was I who brought you up from Egypt and brought you out from the house of slavery.

9 'I delivered you from the hands of the Egyptians and from the hands of all your oppressors, and dispossessed them before you and gave you their land,

10 and I said to you, "I am the LORD your God; you shall not fear the gods of the Amorites in whose land you live. But you have not obeyed Me." ' "

DISCUSS with your GROUP or PONDER on your own . . .

What is Israel's situation at the beginning of Judges 6?

What has Midian been doing to Israel? Note where you marked references to Midian and pay close attention to the verbs that follow.

How does Israel respond?

Who does the LORD send to Israel and what message does he bring?

ONE STEP FURTHER:

Who Are the Midianites?

If you have some extra time this week, see if you can discover what major Old Testament figure the Midianites descended from. Use a concordance or a Bible dictionary to uncover the answer and record below what you find. If you're feeling extra ambitious, also record other run-ins Israel had with the Midianites over the years.

How often do we need to be reminded of all that God has done already to deliver us? Are there ways you regularly remind yourself? Explain.

What kind of circumstances cause you to forget God's goodness? How does our behavior change when we forget about God?

OBSERVE the TEXT of SCRIPTURE

Let's keep moving on to the final portions of Judges 6.

READ Judges 6:11-40 and **MARK** references to *Gideon, the LORD,* and *the men of the city.* Again, be sure to include pronouns.

Judges 6:11-40

11 Then the angel of the LORD came and sat under the oak that was in Ophrah, which belonged to Joash the Abiezrite as his son Gideon was beating out wheat in the wine press in order to save it from the Midianites.

12 The angel of the LORD appeared to him and said to him, "The LORD is with you, O valiant warrior."

13 Then Gideon said to him, "O my lord, if the LORD is with us, why then has all this happened to us? And where are all His miracles which our fathers told us about, saying, 'Did not the LORD bring us up from Egypt?' But now the LORD has abandoned us and given us into the hand of Midian."

14 The LORD looked at him and said, "Go in this your strength and deliver Israel from the hand of Midian. Have I not sent you?"

15 He said to Him, "O Lord, how shall I deliver Israel? Behold, my family is the least in Manasseh, and I am the youngest in my father's house."

16 But the LORD said to him, "Surely I will be with you, and you shall defeat Midian as one man."

17 So Gideon said to Him, "If now I have found favor in Your sight, then show me a sign that it is You who speak with me.

18 "Please do not depart from here, until I come back to You, and bring out my offering and lay it before You." And He said, "I will remain until you return."

19 Then Gideon went in and prepared a young goat and unleavened bread from an ephah of flour; he put the meat in a basket and the broth in a pot, and brought them out to him under the oak and presented them.

20 The angel of God said to him, "Take the meat and the unleavened bread and lay them on this rock, and pour out the broth." And he did so.

21 Then the angel of the LORD put out the end of the staff that was in his hand and touched the meat and the unleavened bread; and fire sprang up from the rock and consumed the meat and the unleavened bread. Then the angel of the LORD vanished from his sight.

22 When Gideon saw that he was the angel of the LORD, he said, "Alas, O Lord GOD! For now I have seen the angel of the LORD face to face."

23 The LORD said to him, "Peace to you, do not fear; you shall not die."

24 Then Gideon built an altar there to the LORD and named it The LORD is Peace. To this day it is still in Ophrah of the Abiezrites.

25 Now on the same night the LORD said to him, "Take your father's bull and a second bull seven years old, and pull down the altar of Baal which belongs to your father, and cut down the Asherah that is beside it;

26 and build an altar to the LORD your God on the top of this stronghold in an orderly manner, and take a second bull and offer a burnt offering with the wood of the Asherah which you shall cut down."

27 Then Gideon took ten men of his servants and did as the LORD had spoken to him; and because he was too afraid of his father's household and the men of the city to do it by day, he did it by night.

28 When the men of the city arose early in the morning, behold, the altar of Baal was torn down, and the Asherah which was beside it was cut down, and the second bull was offered on the altar which had been built.

29 They said to one another, "Who did this thing?" And when they searched about and inquired, they said, "Gideon the son of Joash did this thing."

30 Then the men of the city said to Joash, "Bring out your son, that he may die, for he has torn down the altar of Baal, and indeed, he has cut down the Asherah which was beside it."

31 But Joash said to all who stood against him, "Will you contend for Baal, or will you deliver him? Whoever will plead for him shall be put to death by morning. If he is a god, let him contend for himself, because someone has torn down his altar."

32 Therefore on that day he named him Jerubbaal, that is to say, "Let Baal contend against him," because he had torn down his altar.

FYI:

Rhymes to Remember? Yes!

It may seem corny, but the way I remember who Gideon fought is by way of rhyme. Gideon fought Midian. Whenever a ball is pitched over the plate: HIT IT! Not everything in the Bible is easy to remember, so when it is, consider a rhyme!

33 Then all the Midianites and the Amalekites and the sons of the east assembled themselves; and they crossed over and camped in the valley of Jezreel.

34 So the Spirit of the LORD came upon Gideon; and he blew a trumpet, and the Abiezrites were called together to follow him.

35 He sent messengers throughout Manasseh, and they also were called together to follow him; and he sent messengers to Asher, Zebulun, and Naphtali, and they came up to meet them.

36 Then Gideon said to God, "If You will deliver Israel through me, as You have spoken,

37 behold, I will put a fleece of wool on the threshing floor. If there is dew on the fleece only, and it is dry on all the ground, then I will know that You will deliver Israel through me, as You have spoken."

38 And it was so. When he arose early the next morning and squeezed the fleece, he drained the dew from the fleece, a bowl full of water.

39 Then Gideon said to God, "Do not let Your anger burn against me that I may speak once more; please let me make a test once more with the fleece, let it now be dry only on the fleece, and let there be dew on all the ground."

40 God did so that night; for it was dry only on the fleece, and dew was on all the ground.

DISCUSS with your GROUP or PONDER on your own . . .

What is Gideon doing when the angel of the LORD appears in verse 11? Does the angel's description of Gideon in verse 12 match his behavior?

How does Gideon respond? What questions does he have?

Now, think for a moment. Should Gideon have been able to answer these questions for himself? Why/why not? Where should he have been able to find the answers?

What does the LORD tell Gideon to do?

How does Gideon push back? What does he ask for? What happens?

What sign does Gideon receive and how does he respond?

What does the LORD tell Gideon to do in verse 25?

When and how does Gideon obey? What concerns does he have?

What do "the men of the city" do?

Do you relate with Gideon's fears about the people? How do fears about "the men of [your] city" affect you?

What happens when the Spirit of the LORD comes upon Gideon?

Having already asked for one sign, Gideon now asks for two more. What are they and what does he want to know? How does God respond?

What do you think of his behavior? Explain your thoughts.

Descriptive Versus Prescriptive

As we read through the real-life accounts of the flawed people and leaders in Judges, it is critical that we remember the difference between "description" and "prescription." Description tells us what *did* happen, prescription tells us what *should* happen. Many actions that happened in Judges were neither prescribed nor condoned by God.

DIGGING DEEPER
The Angel of the LORD

If you feel like exercising some brain power this week, see what you can find out about "the angel of the LORD." Here are a few tips to get you started before you address the questions below:
- Use a concordance to search on the phrase "angel of the LORD."
- Note people's reactions after encountering "the angel of the LORD."
- Note when and where "the angel of the LORD" appears and for what purposes.
- Note when "the angel of the LORD" stops appearing.
- Consider other passages, such as Hebrews 1, that provide additional information about angels.

The angel of the LORD could be . . . because . . .

The angel of the LORD can't be . . . because . . .

I think the angel of the LORD is . . . based on . . .

OBSERVE the TEXT of SCRIPTURE

In Judges 7, God's "valiant warrior" gathers troops and engages the Midianite army.

READ Judges 7:1-8 and **MARK** occurrences of the word *deliver* and the phrase *too many*.

Judges 7:1-8

1 Then Jerubbaal (that is, Gideon) and all the people who were with him, rose early and camped beside the spring of Harod; and the camp of Midian was on the north side of them by the hill of Moreh in the valley.

2 The LORD said to Gideon, "The people who are with you are too many for Me to give Midian into their hands, for Israel would become boastful, saying, 'My own power has delivered me.'

3 "Now therefore come, proclaim in the hearing of the people, saying, 'Whoever is afraid and trembling, let him return and depart from Mount Gilead.' " So 22,000 people returned, but 10,000 remained.

4 Then the LORD said to Gideon, "The people are still too many; bring them down to the water and I will test them for you there. Therefore it shall be that he of whom I say to you, 'This one shall go with you,' he shall go with you; but everyone of whom I say to you, 'This one shall not go with you,' he shall not go."

5 So he brought the people down to the water. And the LORD said to Gideon, "You shall separate everyone who laps the water with his tongue as a dog laps, as well as everyone who kneels to drink."

6 Now the number of those who lapped, putting their hand to their mouth, was 300 men; but all the rest of the people kneeled to drink water.

7 The LORD said to Gideon, "I will deliver you with the 300 men who lapped and will give the Midianites into your hands; so let all the other people go, each man to his home."

8 So the 300 men took the people's provisions and their trumpets into their hands. And Gideon sent all the other men of Israel, each to his tent, but retained the 300 men; and the camp of Midian was below him in the valley.

DISCUSS with your GROUP or PONDER on your own . . .

As Judges 7 opens, how many men have responded to Gideon's call for soldiers? What is God's assessment of the number? Why?

How does God prune the number? Why does He choose to deliver through such a small group?

In what ways do we trust in numbers today? How can "numbers" lead our thinking astray? Have they ever led *you* astray? If so, how?

Do you ever become discouraged by numbers? Which ones? How can this account serve as an encouragement?

FYI:

1 > 1,000

"One of your men puts to flight a thousand, for the LORD your God is He who fights for you, just as He promised you. So take diligent heed to yourselves to love the LORD your God."

—Joshua 23:10-11

OBSERVE the TEXT of SCRIPTURE

Let's finish Judges 7.

READ Judges 7:9-25 and **MARK** references to *the LORD*, *Gideon* and *Midian*.

Judges 7:9-25

9 Now the same night it came about that the LORD said to him, "Arise, go down against the camp, for I have given it into your hands.

10 "But if you are afraid to go down, go with Purah your servant down to the camp,

11 and you will hear what they say; and afterward your hands will be strengthened that you may go down against the camp." So he went with Purah his servant down to the outposts of the army that was in the camp.

12 Now the Midianites and the Amalekites and all the sons of the east were lying in the valley as numerous as locusts; and their camels were without number, as numerous as the sand on the seashore.

13 When Gideon came, behold, a man was relating a dream to his friend. And he said, "Behold, I had a dream; a loaf of barley bread was tumbling into the camp of Midian, and it came to the tent and struck it so that it fell, and turned it upside down so that the tent lay flat."

14 His friend replied, "This is nothing less than the sword of Gideon the son of Joash, a man of Israel; God has given Midian and all the camp into his hand."

15 When Gideon heard the account of the dream and its interpretation, he bowed in worship. He returned to the camp of Israel and said, "Arise, for the LORD has given the camp of Midian into your hands."

16 He divided the 300 men into three companies, and he put trumpets and empty pitchers into the hands of all of them, with torches inside the pitchers.

17 He said to them, "Look at me and do likewise. And behold, when I come to the outskirts of the camp, do as I do.

18 "When I and all who are with me blow the trumpet, then you
    also blow the trumpets all around the camp and say, 'For the
    LORD and for Gideon.' "

19 So Gideon and the hundred men who were with him came
    to the outskirts of the camp at the beginning of the middle
    watch, when they had just posted the watch; and they blew the
    trumpets and smashed the pitchers that were in their hands.

20 When the three companies blew the trumpets and broke the
    pitchers, they held the torches in their left hands and the
    trumpets in their right hands for blowing, and cried, "A sword
    for the LORD and for Gideon!"

21 Each stood in his place around the camp; and all the army ran,
    crying out as they fled.

22 When they blew 300 trumpets, the LORD set the sword of one
    against another even throughout the whole army; and the army
    fled as far as Beth-shittah toward Zererah, as far as the edge of
    Abel-meholah, by Tabbath.

23 The men of Israel were summoned from Naphtali and Asher and
    all Manasseh, and they pursued Midian.

24 Gideon sent messengers throughout all the hill country of
    Ephraim, saying, "Come down against Midian and take the
    waters before them, as far as Beth-barah and the Jordan." So all
    the men of Ephraim were summoned and they took the waters
    as far as Beth-barah and the Jordan.

25 They captured the two leaders of Midian, Oreb and Zeeb, and
    they killed Oreb at the rock of Oreb, and they killed Zeeb at the
    wine press of Zeeb, while they pursued Midian; and they brought
    the heads of Oreb and Zeeb to Gideon from across the Jordan.

DISCUSS with your GROUP or PONDER on your own . . .

Why does God send Gideon down to the enemies' camp in verses
9-11?

ONE STEP FURTHER:

How Did It Happen?

The clear, bottom-line answer is that God defeated Midian by causing the Midianites to turn on one another. While we don't need to know specifics to believe this, the text gives us clues that might point to a logical answer. Think through the following questions and see if you can reason to a possible answer:

- When generally did Gideon and his men approach? What time of day?

- Have you ever experienced "true darkness," as in darkness at night apart from ambient city light—a darkness that could be "felt" (Exodus 10:21)? If so, what was it like? If not, ask someone who knows.

- When specifically did Gideon and his men approach? What was happening? How easy would it be to distinguish people in the darkness?

- If you were a Midianite on watch in the dark and heard the racket Gideon's men made, what do you think you would have done if anyone walked by you?

When he arrives, what does he see and hear?

How does Gideon respond in verse 15?

What does Gideon tell the Israelite army to do and say? What does the LORD do? What happens?

Who else is summoned in verses 23-24? How do they help?

OBSERVE the TEXT of SCRIPTURE

Judges 8 reveals a new side of Gideon. Let's take a look.

READ Judges 8. **MARK** every reference to *Gideon*. **UNDERLINE** everything he does.

Judges 8

1   Then the men of Ephraim said to him, "What is this thing you have done to us, not calling us when you went to fight against Midian?" And they contended with him vigorously.

2   But he said to them, "What have I done now in comparison with you? Is not the gleaning of the grapes of Ephraim better than the vintage of Abiezer?

3   "God has given the leaders of Midian, Oreb and Zeeb into your hands; and what was I able to do in comparison with you?" Then their anger toward him subsided when he said that.

4   Then Gideon and the 300 men who were with him came to the Jordan and crossed over, weary yet pursuing.

5   He said to the men of Succoth, "Please give loaves of bread to the people who are following me, for they are weary, and I am pursuing Zebah and Zalmunna, the kings of Midian."

6   The leaders of Succoth said, "Are the hands of Zebah and Zalmunna already in your hands, that we should give bread to your army?"

7   Gideon said, "All right, when the LORD has given Zebah and Zalmunna into my hand, then I will thrash your bodies with the thorns of the wilderness and with briers."

8   He went up from there to Penuel and spoke similarly to them; and the men of Penuel answered him just as the men of Succoth had answered.

9   So he spoke also to the men of Penuel, saying, "When I return safely, I will tear down this tower."

10   Now Zebah and Zalmunna were in Karkor, and their armies with them, about 15,000 men, all who were left of the entire army of the sons of the east; for the fallen were 120,000 swordsmen.

11   Gideon went up by the way of those who lived in tents on the east of Nobah and Jogbehah, and attacked the camp when the camp was unsuspecting.

12 When Zebah and Zalmunna fled, he pursued them and captured the two kings of Midian, Zebah and Zalmunna, and routed the whole army.

13 Then Gideon the son of Joash returned from the battle by the ascent of Heres.

14 And he captured a youth from Succoth and questioned him. Then the youth wrote down for him the princes of Succoth and its elders, seventy-seven men.

15 He came to the men of Succoth and said, "Behold Zebah and Zalmunna, concerning whom you taunted me, saying, 'Are the hands of Zebah and Zalmunna already in your hand, that we should give bread to your men who are weary?' "

16 He took the elders of the city, and thorns of the wilderness and briers, and he disciplined the men of Succoth with them.

17 He tore down the tower of Penuel and killed the men of the city.

18 Then he said to Zebah and Zalmunna, "What kind of men were they whom you killed at Tabor?" And they said, "They were like you, each one resembling the son of a king."

19 He said, "They were my brothers, the sons of my mother. As the LORD lives, if only you had let them live, I would not kill you."

20 So he said to Jether his firstborn, "Rise, kill them." But the youth did not draw his sword, for he was afraid, because he was still a youth.

21 Then Zebah and Zalmunna said, "Rise up yourself, and fall on us; for as the man, so is his strength." So Gideon arose and killed Zebah and Zalmunna, and took the crescent ornaments which were on their camels' necks.

22 Then the men of Israel said to Gideon, "Rule over us, both you and your son, also your son's son, for you have delivered us from the hand of Midian."

23 But Gideon said to them, "I will not rule over you, nor shall my son rule over you; the LORD shall rule over you."

24 Yet Gideon said to them, "I would request of you, that each of you give me an earring from his spoil." (For they had gold earrings, because they were Ishmaelites.)

25 They said, "We will surely give them." So they spread out a garment, and every one of them threw an earring there from his spoil.

26 The weight of the gold earrings that he requested was 1,700 shekels *of gold*, besides the crescent ornaments and the pendants and the purple robes which *were* on the kings of Midian, and besides the neck bands that *were* on their camels' necks.

27 Gideon made it into an ephod, and placed it in his city, Ophrah, and all Israel played the harlot with it there, so that it became a snare to Gideon and his household.

28 So Midian was subdued before the sons of Israel, and they did not lift up their heads anymore. And the land was undisturbed for forty years in the days of Gideon.

29 Then Jerubbaal the son of Joash went and lived in his own house.

30 Now Gideon had seventy sons who were his direct descendants, for he had many wives.

31 His concubine who was in Shechem also bore him a son, and he named him Abimelech.

32 And Gideon the son of Joash died at a ripe old age and was buried in the tomb of his father Joash, in Ophrah of the Abiezrites.

33 Then it came about, as soon as Gideon was dead, that the sons of Israel again played the harlot with the Baals, and made Baal-berith their god.

34 Thus the sons of Israel did not remember the LORD their God, who had delivered them from the hands of all their enemies on every side;

35 nor did they show kindness to the household of Jerubbaal (that is, Gideon) in accord with all the good that he had done to Israel.

DISCUSS with your GROUP or PONDER on your own . . .

Why do the men of Ephraim contend with Gideon in Judges 8:1?

How does Gideon respond? Although Gideon's behavior often leaves much to be desired, what can we learn from him in this encounter?

Do you have any potentially inflammatory situations in your life that you can diffuse with a gentle answer? Explain.

Bearing in mind Gideon's gentle answer to the men of Ephraim, compare his interactions with the men of Succuth and Penuel. What does he ask of these cities? How do they respond? What does he threaten?

What does Gideon do when he finally catches up with the Midianite army?

What does he eventually do to the men of Succuth and Penuel?

How has Gideon changed throughout the account? What high points has he had? Low points? What actions do you think pleased God? Why?

What does Gideon ask Zebah and Zalmunna in verse 18? How do they answer? Why does this matter to Gideon?

After killing the kings of Midian, what does Gideon take from them? (See verses 21 and 26.)

What do the Israelites say to Gideon in verse 22 and how does he respond? (Compare with Judges 7:2 when you answer.) Who was Israel's true deliverer?

Let's consider Gideon's response a little further by breaking it down into what he says and what he does.

WHAT HE SAYS

What do you think of Gideon's response in Judges 8:23 to the people's request for him to rule over them? Do you think he gave a proper, God-honoring answer? Explain.

WHAT HE DOES

Now let's look at Gideon's actions to see if they match his words. Note under each verse reference what Gideon does and compare it with what he has said. Consider the prompts in the parentheses to help you as you answer.

Judges 8:21 *(What did this symbolize? Whose camels wore these ornaments?)*

Judges 8:25 *(What is it called when a population gives a percentage to a governing person or body?)*

Turning Against His Brothers
Both Succoth and Penuel were Israelite cities located in the Transjordan region—the land to the east of the Jordan River.

Judges 8:27 *(What role did the ephod play in Israel? Who wore it? Why?)*

Judges 8:31 *(What does "Abimelech" mean?)*

What do you make of what Gideon says and does—do they match? How would you rate his "finish"? Why?

What can you most relate to in Gideon's story? What have you learned from his faith? From his flaws?

@THE END OF THE DAY . . .

Gideon's confidence shifted throughout his life moving from the hopelessness of "no confidence" to the sweet spot of "God confidence" and eventually to the problem area of "self-confidence." Before you call it a day, spend some time in prayer asking God what you most need to remember from Gideon's life—then write it down so you won't forget.

EXTRA

If you've been working through the EXTRA section, way to go! Keep up the good work! If you haven't, it's not to late to give it a try. Who knows, you might find that it's fun!

Memorize a Key Verse for Each Chapter

Judges 6:14

> *The LORD looked at him and said, "Go in this your strength and deliver Israel from the hand of Midian. Have I not sent you?"*

Judges 7:2

> *The LORD said to Gideon, "The people who are with you are too many for Me to give Midian into their hands, for Israel would become boastful, saying, 'My own power has delivered me.'"*

Judges 8:27

> *Gideon made it into an ephod, and placed it in his city, Ophrah, and all Israel played the harlot with it there, so that it became a snare to Gideon and his household.*

Prefer a different one? Write it down . . .

"Tweet" It

Summarize the message of Judges 6–8 in 140 characters or less.

#Hashtag It

Write a #hashtag for Judges 6.

\#

Write a #hashtag for Judges 7.

\#

Write a #hashtag for Judges 8.

\#

Draw It!

Doodle out the main points or events from Judges 6–8 or sketch out one main point you want to remember.

Leadership Descent

Now Gideon had seventy sons who were his direct descendants, for he had many wives. His concubine who was in Shechem also bore him a son, and he named him Abimelech.
—Judges 8:30-31

After the death of Gideon, while the sons of Israel "again played the harlot with the Baals" (Judges 8:33), one of Gideon's sons decided to make himself king. It's easy to dismiss Abimelech as nothing more than a pride-filled usurper, a blip on the screen of the judges, but his attitude and tactics reflect the fallen heart, a condition that is alive and well today. Those who want to be king—albeit of their own tiny kingdoms—still live among us! Sometimes, if we're honest, we see them in the mirror.

REMEMBERING

Take a few minutes to summarize Judges 1–8. Be brief.

What has been your biggest application point so far? How is what you're learning changing the way you think and act?

OBSERVE the TEXT of SCRIPTURE

Judges 9 is *the longest chapter* in Judges. It's huge, but realize that once you make it through, everything from here on out gets easier. We'll tackle it segment-by-segment so it will be manageable.

READ Judges 9:1-6 and **MARK** references to *Abimelech* including pronouns.

Judges 9:1-6

1 *And Abimelech the son of Jerubbaal went to Shechem to his mother's relatives, and spoke to them and to the whole clan of the household of his mother's father, saying,*

2 *"Speak, now, in the hearing of all the leaders of Shechem, 'Which is better for you, that seventy men, all the sons of Jerubbaal, rule over you, or that one man rule over you?' Also, remember that I am your bone and your flesh."*

3 *And his mother's relatives spoke all these words on his behalf in the hearing of all the leaders of Shechem; and they were inclined to follow Abimelech, for they said, "He is our relative."*

4 *They gave him seventy pieces of silver from the house of Baal-berith with which Abimelech hired worthless and reckless fellows, and they followed him.*

5 Then he went to his father's house at Ophrah and killed his brothers the sons of Jerubbaal, seventy men, on one stone. But Jotham the youngest son of Jerubbaal was left, for he hid himself.

6 All the men of Shechem and all Beth-millo assembled together, and they went and made Abimelech king, by the oak of the pillar which was in Shechem.

DISCUSS with your GROUP or PONDER on your own . . .

What have we learned about Abimelech prior to Judges 9?

Upon the death of Gideon, what does Abimelech want? How does he maneuver to get it?

What pitch does he make to the people of Shechem? How do they respond?

How does he obtain "working capital" and what does he do with it?

Not Part of the Family
While Gideon and his wives lived in Ophrah, his concubine—the mother of Abimelech—was from Shechem. It is likely that she was a Canaanite.

Having obtained support from his mother's side of the family, what did Abimelech do to his father's side? What does this say about his character? Is this the kind of man who should be a ruler? Explain your answer.

How does self-raised Abimelech's character differ from that of the judges God had raised up?

If you are in a position of leadership, what is the condition of your heart? Are you seeking God's purposes or your own? How can you tell the difference?

OBSERVE the TEXT of SCRIPTURE

READ Judges 9:7-22 and **MARK** references to *truth* and *integrity*.

Judges 9:7-22

7 *Now when they told Jotham, he went and stood on the top of Mount Gerizim, and lifted his voice and called out. Thus he said to them, "Listen to me, O men of Shechem, that God may listen to you.*

8 *"Once the trees went forth to anoint a king over them, and they said to the olive tree, 'Reign over us!'*

9 *"But the olive tree said to them, 'Shall I leave my fatness with which God and men are honored, and go to wave over the trees?'*

10 *"Then the trees said to the fig tree, 'You come, reign over us!'*

11 "But the fig tree said to them, 'Shall I leave my sweetness and my good fruit, and go to wave over the trees?'

12 "Then the trees said to the vine, 'You come, reign over us!'

13 "But the vine said to them, 'Shall I leave my new wine, which cheers God and men, and go to wave over the trees?'

14 "Finally all the trees said to the bramble, 'You come, reign over us!'

15 "The bramble said to the trees, 'If in truth you are anointing me as king over you, come and take refuge in my shade; but if not, may fire come out from the bramble and consume the cedars of Lebanon.'

16 "Now therefore, if you have dealt in truth and integrity in making Abimelech king, and if you have dealt well with Jerubbaal and his house, and have dealt with him as he deserved—

17 for my father fought for you and risked his life and delivered you from the hand of Midian;

18 but you have risen against my father's house today and have killed his sons, seventy men, on one stone, and have made Abimelech, the son of his maidservant, king over the men of Shechem, because he is your relative—

19 if then you have dealt in truth and integrity with Jerubbaal and his house this day, rejoice in Abimelech, and let him also rejoice in you.

20 "But if not, let fire come out from Abimelech and consume the men of Shechem and Beth-millo; and let fire come out from the men of Shechem and from Beth-millo, and consume Abimelech."

21 Then Jotham escaped and fled, and went to Beer and remained there because of Abimelech his brother.

22 Now Abimelech ruled over Israel three years.

DISCUSS with your GROUP or PONDER on your own . . .

Who is Jotham and what does he do?

ONE STEP FURTHER:

What is Bramble?

If you have some time this week, find the Hebrew word for "bramble" and see what you can learn about the plant Jotham refers to in his speech. Record below what you discover.

Let's look at the message Jotham brings to Abimelech's relatives in Shechem in the form of a fable.

- What do "the trees" want?

- Who are the first three candidates they ask to fill the position and why does each turn them down?

1.

2.

3.

- Who finally accepts?

What is Jotham saying about Abimelech through this fable?

How does Jotham challenge the men of Shechem regarding truth and integrity? Why does he take issue with them?

OBSERVE the TEXT of SCRIPTURE

READ Judges 9:23-49 and **MARK** references to *the men of Shechem.*

Judges 9:23-49

23 Then God sent an evil spirit between Abimelech and the men of Shechem; and the men of Shechem dealt treacherously with Abimelech,

24 so that the violence done to the seventy sons of Jerubbaal might come, and their blood might be laid on Abimelech their brother, who killed them, and on the men of Shechem, who strengthened his hands to kill his brothers.

25 The men of Shechem set men in ambush against him on the tops of the mountains, and they robbed all who might pass by them along the road; and it was told to Abimelech.

26 Now Gaal the son of Ebed came with his relatives, and crossed over into Shechem; and the men of Shechem put their trust in him.

27 They went out into the field and gathered the grapes of their vineyards and trod them, and held a festival; and they went into the house of their god, and ate and drank and cursed Abimelech.

FYI:

The Meaning of His Name

Abimelech's name contains two Hebrew words: *ab* (father) and *melek* (king)—"my father [is] king." You may have noticed that the name Abimelech is also associated with the rulers of the Philistines during the time of Abraham and Isaac and used as a title, much like "Pharaoh" referred to a position rather than to a specific person.

28   Then Gaal the son of Ebed said, "Who is Abimelech, and who is
     Shechem, that we should serve him? Is he not the son of Jerubbaal,
     and is Zebul not his lieutenant? Serve the men of Hamor the father
     of Shechem; but why should we serve him?

29   "Would, therefore, that this people were under my authority! Then
     I would remove Abimelech." And he said to Abimelech, "Increase
     your army and come out."

30   When Zebul the ruler of the city heard the words of Gaal the son of
     Ebed, his anger burned.

31   He sent messengers to Abimelech deceitfully, saying, "Behold,
     Gaal the son of Ebed and his relatives have come to Shechem; and
     behold, they are stirring up the city against you.

32   "Now therefore, arise by night, you and the people who are with
     you, and lie in wait in the field.

33   "In the morning, as soon as the sun is up, you shall rise early and
     rush upon the city; and behold, when he and the people who are
     with him come out against you, you shall do to them whatever you
     can."

34   So Abimelech and all the people who were with him arose by night
     and lay in wait against Shechem in four companies.

35   Now Gaal the son of Ebed went out and stood in the entrance of
     the city gate; and Abimelech and the people who were with him
     arose from the ambush.

36   When Gaal saw the people, he said to Zebul, "Look, people are
     coming down from the tops of the mountains." But Zebul said to
     him, "You are seeing the shadow of the mountains as if they were
     men."

37   Gaal spoke again and said, "Behold, people are coming down from
     the highest part of the land, and one company comes by the way of
     the diviners' oak."

FYI:

Using Commentaries

Commentaries are helpful tools to use after you've done your own study. An excellent one-volume
commentary on the Bible is The Moody's Bible Commentary edited by Dr. Michael Rydelnik and Dr.
Michael Vanlaningham.

38 Then Zebul said to him, "Where is your boasting now with which
you said, 'Who is Abimelech that we should serve him?' Is this not
the people whom you despised? Go out now and fight with them!"

39 So Gaal went out before the leaders of Shechem and fought with
Abimelech.

40 Abimelech chased him, and he fled before him; and many fell
wounded up to the entrance of the gate.

41 Then Abimelech remained at Arumah, but Zebul drove out Gaal
and his relatives so that they could not remain in Shechem.

42 Now it came about the next day, that the people went out to the
field, and it was told to Abimelech.

43 So he took his people and divided them into three companies, and
lay in wait in the field; when he looked and saw the people coming
out from the city, he arose against them and slew them.

44 Then Abimelech and the company who was with him dashed
forward and stood in the entrance of the city gate; the other two
companies then dashed against all who were in the field and slew
them.

45 Abimelech fought against the city all that day, and he captured the
city and killed the people who were in it; then he razed the city and
sowed it with salt.

46 When all the leaders of the tower of Shechem heard of it, they
entered the inner chamber of the temple of El-berith.

47 It was told Abimelech that all the leaders of the tower of Shechem
were gathered together.

48 So Abimelech went up to Mount Zalmon, he and all the people
who were with him; and Abimelech took an axe in his hand and
cut down a branch from the trees, and lifted it and laid it on his
shoulder. Then he said to the people who were with him, "What
you have seen me do, hurry and do likewise."

49 All the people also cut down each one his branch and followed
Abimelech, and put them on the inner chamber and set the inner
chamber on fire over those inside, so that all the men of the tower
of Shechem also died, about a thousand men and women.

DISCUSS with your GROUP or PONDER on your own . . .

How does the arrangement between Abimelech and the men of Shechem change and why?

What new character enters the scene? How does he compare with Abimelech? What is his pitch to the people? Why does he say they should follow him instead of Abimelech?

Who is Zebul? How do he and Abimelech rid themselves of Gaal and his threat?

What does Abimelech then do to the city of Shechem? (Remember, these were his relatives.) Does this remind you of how he has dealt with relatives who crossed him before?

Who is Hamor?

Hamor was the father of Shechem. In attaching his lineage to Hamor, Gaal one-ups Abimelech's "relative" claim by going back a generation. Abimelech may have relatives in the city, but Gaal claims to be from the true original stock . . . which also suggests that he is fully Canaanite!

OBSERVE the TEXT of SCRIPTURE

READ Judges 9:50-57 and **MARK** references to *God*.

Judges 9:50-57

50 *Then Abimelech went to Thebez, and he camped against Thebez and captured it.*

51 *But there was a strong tower in the center of the city, and all the men and women with all the leaders of the city fled there and shut themselves in; and they went up on the roof of the tower.*

52 *So Abimelech came to the tower and fought against it, and approached the entrance of the tower to burn it with fire.*

53 *But a certain woman threw an upper millstone on Abimelech's head, crushing his skull.*

54 *Then he called quickly to the young man, his armor bearer, and said to him, "Draw your sword and kill me, so that it will not be said of me, 'A woman slew him.' " So the young man pierced him through, and he died.*

55 *When the men of Israel saw that Abimelech was dead, each departed to his home.*

56 *Thus God repaid the wickedness of Abimelech, which he had done to his father in killing his seventy brothers.*

57 *Also God returned all the wickedness of the men of Shechem on their heads, and the curse of Jotham the son of Jerubbaal came upon them.*

DISCUSS with your GROUP or PONDER on your own . . .

What happens at Thebez?

How does Abimelech die?

What does he *not* want to be said of him? What *are* we saying about him today?

How does God work in this entire situation? Pay close attention to verses 56 and 57.

What takeaways are there for us in knowing that God can and will act?

Do you have any specific situations in your life now where you need to trust God to act instead of taking matters into your own hands? Explain.

How do you deal with the tension between "rising up as a mother in Israel" (as Deborah did) and waiting for God to act against wickedness?

OBSERVE the TEXT of SCRIPTURE

Judges 10 introduces two minor judges and records Israel's continuing pattern of idolatry and rebellion.

READ Judges 10 and **MARK** references to *the sons of Israel* and *the LORD*.

Judges 10

1   Now after Abimelech died, Tola the son of Puah, the son of Dodo, a man of Issachar, arose to save Israel; and he lived in Shamir in the hill country of Ephraim.

2   He judged Israel twenty-three years. Then he died and was buried in Shamir.

3   After him, Jair the Gileadite arose and judged Israel twenty-two years.

4   He had thirty sons who rode on thirty donkeys, and they had thirty cities in the land of Gilead that are called Havvoth-jair to this day.

5   And Jair died and was buried in Kamon.

6   Then the sons of Israel again did evil in the sight of the LORD, served the Baals and the Ashtaroth, the gods of Aram, the gods of Sidon, the gods of Moab, the gods of the sons of Ammon, and the gods of the Philistines; thus they forsook the LORD and did not serve Him.

7   The anger of the LORD burned against Israel, and He sold them into the hands of the Philistines and into the hands of the sons of Ammon.

8   They afflicted and crushed the sons of Israel that year; for eighteen years they afflicted all the sons of Israel who were beyond the Jordan in Gilead in the land of the Amorites.

9   The sons of Ammon crossed the Jordan to fight also against Judah, Benjamin, and the house of Ephraim, so that Israel was greatly distressed.

10 Then the sons of Israel cried out to the LORD, saying, "We have sinned against You, for indeed, we have forsaken our God and served the Baals."

11 The LORD said to the sons of Israel, "Did I not deliver you from the Egyptians, the Amorites, the sons of Ammon, and the Philistines?

12 *"Also when the Sidonians, the Amalekites and the Maonites oppressed you, you cried out to Me, and I delivered you from their hands.*

13 *"Yet you have forsaken Me and served other gods; therefore I will no longer deliver you.*

14 *"Go and cry out to the gods which you have chosen; let them deliver you in the time of your distress."*

15 *The sons of Israel said to the LORD, "We have sinned, do to us whatever seems good to You; only please deliver us this day."*

16 *So they put away the foreign gods from among them and served the LORD; and He could bear the misery of Israel no longer.*

17 *Then the sons of Ammon were summoned and they camped in Gilead. And the sons of Israel gathered together and camped in Mizpah.*

18 *The people, the leaders of Gilead, said to one another, "Who is the man who will begin to fight against the sons of Ammon? He shall become head over all the inhabitants of Gilead."*

DISCUSS with your GROUP or PONDER on your own . . .

What "minor" judges follow the Abimelech incident? What do we know about them?

What cycle begins again after the death of the Jair? How extensive has Israel's idolatry become? How do you know this?

What enemies come against them this time?

> **Gilead**
> Gilead is east of the Jordan River, inhabited by Reuben, Gad, and the half-tribe of Manasseh.

How does the LORD respond to their cries for help this time? Compare this to His previous responses to their cries.

What happens in verses 15-18? What do the Gileadites need and how do they go about filling it?

OBSERVE the TEXT of SCRIPTURE

Thanks for hanging in there! We have two more chapters to go, but they're significantly shorter.

READ Judges 11:1-11 and **MARK** references to *Jephthah.*

Judges 11:1-11

1 *Now Jephthah the Gileadite was a valiant warrior, but he was the son of a harlot. And Gilead was the father of Jephthah.*

2 *Gilead's wife bore him sons; and when his wife's sons grew up, they drove Jephthah out and said to him, "You shall not have an inheritance in our father's house, for you are the son of another woman."*

3 *So Jephthah fled from his brothers and lived in the land of Tob; and worthless fellows gathered themselves about Jephthah, and they went out with him.*

4 *It came about after a while that the sons of Ammon fought against Israel.*

5 When the sons of Ammon fought against Israel, the elders of Gilead went to get Jephthah from the land of Tob;

6 and they said to Jephthah, "Come and be our chief that we may fight against the sons of Ammon."

7 Then Jephthah said to the elders of Gilead, "Did you not hate me and drive me from my father's house? So why have you come to me now when you are in trouble?"

8 The elders of Gilead said to Jephthah, "For this reason we have now returned to you, that you may go with us and fight with the sons of Ammon and become head over all the inhabitants of Gilead."

9 So Jephthah said to the elders of Gilead, "If you take me back to fight against the sons of Ammon and the LORD gives them up to me, will I become your head?"

10 The elders of Gilead said to Jephthah, "The LORD is witness between us; surely we will do as you have said."

11 Then Jephthah went with the elders of Gilead, and the people made him head and chief over them; and Jephthah spoke all his words before the LORD at Mizpah.

DISCUSS with your GROUP or PONDER on your own . . .

Who is Jephthah? How does the text describe him?

Does Jephthah remind you of anyone? If so, who and in what ways?

Why do the elders of Gilead approach Jephthah?

ONE STEP FURTHER:

Who are the Ammonites?

If you have some time this week, see what you can discover about the Ammonites. Who is their forefather? Are they related to the Israelites in any way? What is their history? Record below what you discover.

How does Jephthah respond to them? What does he negotiate for?

Does God play a role in any of the proceedings? If so, how and where?

OBSERVE the TEXT of SCRIPTURE

READ Judges 11:12-28 and continue to **MARK** references to *Jephthah*. Also **MARK** references to *the LORD*.

Judges 11:12-28

12 Now Jephthah sent messengers to the king of the sons of Ammon, saying, "What is between you and me, that you have come to me to fight against my land?"

13 The king of the sons of Ammon said to the messengers of Jephthah, "Because Israel took away my land when they came up from Egypt, from the Arnon as far as the Jabbok and the Jordan; therefore, return them peaceably now."

14 *But Jephthah sent messengers again to the king of the sons of Ammon,*

15 *and they said to him, "Thus says Jephthah, 'Israel did not take away the land of Moab nor the land of the sons of Ammon.*

16 *'For when they came up from Egypt, and Israel went through the wilderness to the Red Sea and came to Kadesh,*

17 *then Israel sent messengers to the king of Edom, saying, "Please let us pass through your land," but the king of Edom would not listen. And they also sent to the king of Moab, but he would not consent. So Israel remained at Kadesh.*

18 *'Then they went through the wilderness and around the land of Edom and the land of Moab, and came to the east side of the land of Moab, and they camped beyond the Arnon; but they did not enter the territory of Moab, for the Arnon was the border of Moab.*

19 *'And Israel sent messengers to Sihon king of the Amorites, the king of Heshbon, and Israel said to him, "Please let us pass through your land to our place."*

20 *'But Sihon did not trust Israel to pass through his territory; so Sihon gathered all his people and camped in Jahaz and fought with Israel.*

21 *'The LORD, the God of Israel, gave Sihon and all his people into the hand of Israel, and they defeated them; so Israel possessed all the land of the Amorites, the inhabitants of that country.*

22 *'So they possessed all the territory of the Amorites, from the Arnon as far as the Jabbok, and from the wilderness as far as the Jordan.*

23 *'Since now the LORD, the God of Israel, drove out the Amorites from before His people Israel, are you then to possess it?*

24 *'Do you not possess what Chemosh your god gives you to possess? So whatever the LORD our God has driven out before us, we will possess it.*

25 *'Now are you any better than Balak the son of Zippor, king of Moab? Did he ever strive with Israel, or did he ever fight against them?*

26 *'While Israel lived in Heshbon and its villages, and in Aroer and its villages, and in all the cities that are on the banks of the Arnon, three hundred years, why did you not recover them within that time?*

27 '*I therefore have not sinned against you, but you are doing me wrong by making war against me; may the LORD, the Judge, judge today between the sons of Israel and the sons of Ammon.'* "

28 *But the king of the sons of Ammon disregarded the message which Jephthah sent him.*

DISCUSS with your GROUP or PONDER on your own . . .

How does Jephthah engage the Ammonites?

What is the point of contention between the two groups? How far back does it go?

What argument does Jephthah make regarding Israel's right to the land? Who gave the land to Israel? Who does he appeal to?

How do the negotiations go? Does Ammon give in?

OBSERVE the TEXT of SCRIPTURE

READ Judges 11:29-40 and **MARK** references to Jephthah's *daughter* and to *virginity*.

Judges 11:29-40

29 *Now the Spirit of the LORD came upon Jephthah, so that he passed through Gilead and Manasseh; then he passed through Mizpah of Gilead, and from Mizpah of Gilead he went on to the sons of Ammon.*

30 *Jephthah made a vow to the LORD and said, "If You will indeed give the sons of Ammon into my hand,*

31 *then it shall be that whatever comes out of the doors of my house to meet me when I return in peace from the sons of Ammon, it shall be the LORD'S, and I will offer it up as a burnt offering."*

32 *So Jephthah crossed over to the sons of Ammon to fight against them; and the LORD gave them into his hand.*

33 *He struck them with a very great slaughter from Aroer to the entrance of Minnith, twenty cities, and as far as Abel-keramim. So the sons of Ammon were subdued before the sons of Israel.*

34 *When Jephthah came to his house at Mizpah, behold, his daughter was coming out to meet him with tambourines and with dancing. Now she was his one and only child; besides her he had no son or daughter.*

35 *When he saw her, he tore his clothes and said, "Alas, my daughter! You have brought me very low, and you are among those who trouble me; for I have given my word to the LORD, and I cannot take it back."*

36 *So she said to him, "My father, you have given your word to the LORD; do to me as you have said, since the LORD has avenged you of your enemies, the sons of Ammon."*

37 *She said to her father, "Let this thing be done for me; let me alone two months, that I may go to the mountains and weep because of my virginity, I and my companions."*

38 *Then he said, "Go." So he sent her away for two months; and she left with her companions, and wept on the mountains because of her virginity.*

39 *At the end of two months she returned to her father, who did to her according to the vow which he had made; and she had no relations with a man. Thus it became a custom in Israel,*

40 *that the daughters of Israel went yearly to commemorate the daughter of Jephthah the Gileadite four days in the year.*

DISCUSS with your GROUP or PONDER on your own . . .

What happens to Jephthah and what does he do in response in verse 29?

What does Jephthah vow to the LORD in verses 30-31? Is there anything in Jephthah's character or history that this is consistent with? (Think about his interactions with the men of Gilead.)

Have you ever known someone to say, "God, if you give me this, then I'll do that"? What do you make of this?

Have *you* ever tried bargaining with God? How did that work for you?

Did God ask Jephthah to make a vow? What help had God already given him? Why is God helping them?

What happens in the battle? Who comes out of the house to meet Jephthah upon his return? What are we told about her?

What happens next? What does Jephthah do? What does his daughter do?

While you'd almost certainly never make Jephthah's vow, do you ever struggle with rash words? Where have they taken you? How can what you know about God help you to choose better?

Moving on . . .

OBSERVE the TEXT of SCRIPTURE

As you read, remember that Ephraim is located on the west side of the Jordan River and the Gileadites are located on the east side of it.

READ Judges and **MARK** references to *the men of Ephraim*. Be sure to include pronouns.

Judges 12

1   Then the men of Ephraim were summoned, and they crossed to Zaphon and said to Jephthah, "Why did you cross over to fight against the sons of Ammon without calling us to go with you? We will burn your house down on you."

2   Jephthah said to them, "I and my people were at great strife with the sons of Ammon; when I called you, you did not deliver me from their hand.

3   "When I saw that you would not deliver me, I took my life in my hands and crossed over against the sons of Ammon, and the LORD gave them into my hand. Why then have you come up to me this day to fight against me?"

4   Then Jephthah gathered all the men of Gilead and fought Ephraim; and the men of Gilead defeated Ephraim, because they said, "You are fugitives of Ephraim, O Gileadites, in the midst of Ephraim and in the midst of Manasseh."

5   The Gileadites captured the fords of the Jordan opposite Ephraim. And it happened when any of the fugitives of Ephraim said, "Let me cross over," the men of Gilead would say to him, "Are you an Ephraimite?" If he said, "No,"

6   then they would say to him, "Say now, 'Shibboleth.' " But he said, "Sibboleth," for he could not pronounce it correctly. Then they seized him and slew him at the fords of the Jordan. Thus there fell at that time 42,000 of Ephraim.

7   Jephthah judged Israel six years. Then Jephthah the Gileadite died and was buried in one of the cities of Gilead.

8   Now Ibzan of Bethlehem judged Israel after him.

9   He had thirty sons, and thirty daughters whom he gave in marriage outside the family, and he brought in thirty daughters from outside for his sons. And he judged Israel seven years.

10   Then Ibzan died and was buried in Bethlehem.

11   Now Elon the Zebulunite judged Israel after him; and he judged Israel ten years.

12   Then Elon the Zebulunite died and was buried at Aijalon in the land of Zebulun.

13   Now Abdon the son of Hillel the Pirathonite judged Israel after him.

14   He had forty sons and thirty grandsons who rode on seventy donkeys; and he judged Israel eight years.

15   Then Abdon the son of Hillel the Pirathonite died and was buried at Pirathon in the land of Ephraim, in the hill country of the Amalekites.

DISCUSS with your GROUP or PONDER on your own . . .

What are the men of Ephraim upset about at the beginning of Judges 12?

How does Jephthah respond? Compare this with Gideon's response when the men of Ephraim were upset with him.

On which side of the Jordan River does the conversation in Judges 12:1-3 take place? Why is this significant?

How do the visiting Ephraimites taunt the men of Gilead in verse 4?

How do the Gileadites then capture the Ephraimites who are in their land according to verse 5?

Who should these men be fighting? Yet, who *are* they fighting?

What does in-fighting reveal about the heart of any group be it a nation, a church, or another kind of organization? What does this specific incident reveal about Israel?

What judges arise after Jephthah dies? What do we learn about them?

@THE END OF THE DAY . . .

There's been SO much narrative this week that it can be easy for us to be swallowed up by the story and forget to apply what we've learned . . . but we're not going to do that. Spend some time going back over what we've studied chapter-by-chapter and writing down one key truth or action item for each.

Truth/Action Item for Judges 9:

Truth/Action Item for Judges 10:

Truth/Action Item for Judges 11:

Truth/Action Item for Judges 12:

EXTRA
MEMORIZE | TWEET | POST | DRAW | HASHTAG | ENCODE | REMEMBER

I hesitate to even include this, given the length of this lesson!

Pick and Memorize a Key Verse for Each Chapter

Judges 9

Judges 10

Judges 11

Judges 12

"Tweet" It

Summarize the message of Judges 9 in 140 characters or less.

Summarize the message of Judges 10 in 140 characters or less.

Summarize the message of Judges 11 in 140 characters or less.

Summarize the message of Judges 12 in 140 characters or less.

#Hashtag It

Write a #hashtag for Judges 9.

#

Write a #hashtag for Judges 10.

#

Write a #hashtag for Judges 11.

#

Write a #hashtag for Judges 12.

#

"Right in My Eyes"

But Samson said to his father,
"Get her for me, for she looks good to me."
—Judges 14:3b

Who among us hasn't found someone or something attractive or desirable based on looks alone? But experiencing attraction and impulsively chasing are two different animals. As we come to the account of the final recorded judge in this book, we'll see how far Israel has fallen from the time of Joshua and even from the time of the good judge Othniel.

REMEMBERING

Briefly summarize the basics from each chapter we've studied so far and add your biggest application action items. Remember, if we're just observing and interpreting we're missing the end goal of applying the Word. We need always to apply to *our* lives the truths that we're learning!

	Main Truths/Key Words #Hashtags!	My Application
Judges 1–2		
Judges 3		
Judges 4–5		
Judges 6–8		
Judges 9		
Judges 10–12		

OBSERVE the TEXT of SCRIPTURE

READ Judges 13 and **MARK** every reference to *Manoah*, his *wife*, and the *angel of the LORD*. Be sure to include pronouns and synonyms.

Judges 13

1 Now the sons of Israel again did evil in the sight of the LORD, so that the LORD gave them into the hands of the Philistines forty years.

2 There was a certain man of Zorah, of the family of the Danites, whose name was Manoah; and his wife was barren and had borne no children.

3 Then the angel of the LORD appeared to the woman and said to her, "Behold now, you are barren and have borne no children, but you shall conceive and give birth to a son.

4 "Now therefore, be careful not to drink wine or strong drink, nor eat any unclean thing.

5 *"For behold, you shall conceive and give birth to a son, and no razor shall come upon his head, for the boy shall be a Nazirite to God from the womb; and he shall begin to deliver Israel from the hands of the Philistines."*

6 *Then the woman came and told her husband, saying, "A man of God came to me and his appearance was like the appearance of the angel of God, very awesome. And I did not ask him where he came from, nor did he tell me his name.*

7 *"But he said to me, 'Behold, you shall conceive and give birth to a son, and now you shall not drink wine or strong drink nor eat any unclean thing, for the boy shall be a Nazirite to God from the womb to the day of his death.' "*

8 *Then Manoah entreated the LORD and said, "O Lord, please let the man of God whom You have sent come to us again that he may teach us what to do for the boy who is to be born."*

9 *God listened to the voice of Manoah; and the angel of God came again to the woman as she was sitting in the field, but Manoah her husband was not with her.*

10 *So the woman ran quickly and told her husband, "Behold, the man who came the other day has appeared to me."*

11 *Then Manoah arose and followed his wife, and when he came to the man he said to him, "Are you the man who spoke to the woman?" And he said, "I am."*

12 *Manoah said, "Now when your words come to pass, what shall be the boy's mode of life and his vocation?"*

13 *So the angel of the LORD said to Manoah, "Let the woman pay attention to all that I said.*

14 *"She should not eat anything that comes from the vine nor drink wine or strong drink, nor eat any unclean thing; let her observe all that I commanded."*

15 *Then Manoah said to the angel of the LORD, "Please let us detain you so that we may prepare a young goat for you."*

16 *The angel of the LORD said to Manoah, "Though you detain me, I will not eat your food, but if you prepare a burnt offering, then offer it to the LORD." For Manoah did not know that he was the angel of the LORD.*

17 Manoah said to the angel of the LORD, "What is your name, so that when your words come to pass, we may honor you?"

18 But the angel of the LORD said to him, "Why do you ask my name, seeing it is wonderful?"

19 So Manoah took the young goat with the grain offering and offered it on the rock to the LORD, and He performed wonders while Manoah and his wife looked on.

20 For it came about when the flame went up from the altar toward heaven, that the angel of the LORD ascended in the flame of the altar. When Manoah and his wife saw this, they fell on their faces to the ground.

21 Now the angel of the LORD did not appear to Manoah or his wife again. Then Manoah knew that he was the angel of the LORD.

22 So Manoah said to his wife, "We will surely die, for we have seen God."

23 But his wife said to him, "If the LORD had desired to kill us, He would not have accepted a burnt offering and a grain offering from our hands, nor would He have shown us all these things, nor would He have let us hear things like this at this time."

24 Then the woman gave birth to a son and named him Samson; and the child grew up and the LORD blessed him.

25 And the Spirit of the LORD began to stir him in Mahaneh-dan, between Zorah and Eshtaol.

DISCUSS with your GROUP or PONDER on your own . . .

What has Israel done at the beginning of Judges 13 and what situation has it gotten them into?

What part of the expected "cycle" is missing in this account? Why do you think that might be?

Who is Manoah? List what you know about him from the text.

Describe Manoah's wife. What facts did you learn about her?

Who does the angel of the LORD appear to and what message does he bring?

ONE STEP FURTHER:

Birth Announcements

If you have some extra time this week, see if you can find out what other biblical characters had "angelic" birth announcements. You'll find others in both the Old and New Testaments. Record below what you discover.

ONE STEP FURTHER:

Danites

Take some time this week to see what you can find out about the tribe of Dan. They will show up again in our lesson next week! Be sure to pay close attention to where they are settled at different times and why they are where they are.

How does Manoah's wife respond?

How does she describe the angel of the LORD?

How does Manoah respond when his wife tells him about the angel of the LORD?

Why does the angel of the LORD appear a second time? What happens when he appears?

Who do you think the angel of the LORD is? Explain your answer from Scripture.

OBSERVE the TEXT of SCRIPTURE

READ Judges 14 and **MARK** every reference to eyes/seeing/looking, etc.

Judges 14

1 Then Samson went down to Timnah and saw a woman in Timnah, one of the daughters of the Philistines.

2 So he came back and told his father and mother, "I saw a woman in Timnah, one of the daughters of the Philistines; now therefore, get her for me as a wife."

3 Then his father and his mother said to him, "Is there no woman among the daughters of your relatives, or among all our people, that you go to take a wife from the uncircumcised Philistines?" But Samson said to his father, "Get her for me, for she looks good to me."

4 However, his father and mother did not know that it was of the LORD, for He was seeking an occasion against the Philistines. Now at that time the Philistines were ruling over Israel.

5 Then Samson went down to Timnah with his father and mother, and came as far as the vineyards of Timnah; and behold, a young lion came roaring toward him.

6 The Spirit of the LORD came upon him mightily, so that he tore him as one tears a young goat though he had nothing in his hand; but he did not tell his father or mother what he had done.

7   So he went down and talked to the woman; and she looked good to Samson.

8   When he returned later to take her, he turned aside to look at the carcass of the lion; and behold, a swarm of bees and honey were in the body of the lion.

9   So he scraped the honey into his hands and went on, eating as he went. When he came to his father and mother, he gave some to them and they ate it; but he did not tell them that he had scraped the honey out of the body of the lion.

10   Then his father went down to the woman; and Samson made a feast there, for the young men customarily did this.

11   When they saw him, they brought thirty companions to be with him.

12   Then Samson said to them, "Let me now propound a riddle to you; if you will indeed tell it to me within the seven days of the feast, and find it out, then I will give you thirty linen wraps and thirty changes of clothes.

13   "But if you are unable to tell me, then you shall give me thirty linen wraps and thirty changes of clothes." And they said to him, "Propound your riddle, that we may hear it."

14   So he said to them, "Out of the eater came something to eat, And out of the strong came something sweet." But they could not tell the riddle in three days.

15   Then it came about on the fourth day that they said to Samson's wife, "Entice your husband, so that he will tell us the riddle, or we will burn you and your father's house with fire. Have you invited us to impoverish us? Is this not so?"

16   Samson's wife wept before him and said, "You only hate me, and you do not love me; you have propounded a riddle to the sons of my people, and have not told it to me." And he said to her, "Behold, I have not told it to my father or mother; so should I tell you?"

17   However she wept before him seven days while their feast lasted. And on the seventh day he told her because she pressed him so hard. She then told the riddle to the sons of her people.

18 So the men of the city said to him on the seventh day before
the sun went down, "What is sweeter than honey? And what is
stronger than a lion?" And he said to them, "If you had not plowed
with my heifer, You would not have found out my riddle."

19 Then the Spirit of the LORD came upon him mightily, and he went
down to Ashkelon and killed thirty of them and took their spoil and
gave the changes of clothes to those who told the riddle. And his
anger burned, and he went up to his father's house.

20 But Samson's wife was given to his companion who had been his
friend.

DISCUSS with your GROUP or PONDER on your own . . .

Approximately how much time passes between Judges 13 and 14?

Describe the political situation of the day? Are the Israelite's doing
anything about it? Why/why not?

What does Samson want according to the beginning of Judges 14? How
does this align with God's revealed will to His people? How does he try to
involve his parents?

How do Samson's parents react to his demand for the Philistine wife?

List every reference to Samson's eyes/vision in verses 1-9. What impact does his vision have on him?

In spite of Samson's actions, what does verse 4 say the LORD is planning?

What happens to Samson on his way to Timnah in verses 5-6?

Can you think of any reason he would not tell his parents what had happened? Explain.

What happens when Samson returns to Timnah? What does he find according to verses 8-9? What does he do? What is the problem?

DIGGING DEEPER
Where Should Our Eyes Be Set?

Throughout the account we just read, Samson's eyes (and hence his mind) wandered to things of this world. Take some time this week to consider what we as believers should be setting our minds on and what we should be seeking. I'll give you a couple of places to start looking, but see what else you can discover on your own using a combination of your memory and a concordance!

Deuteronomy 6:5ff

Hebrews 12:1-3

Describe the wedding feast and the activities that take place.

Do you think Samson's riddle is fair? Why/why not?

How do the Philistines eventually answer the riddle? What do they threaten?

How does Samson pay his debt?

What did you learn from this account about Samson's character? Record as many specific examples as you noticed.

Where is Samson at the end of the chapter? What happens to his wife?

OBSERVE the TEXT of SCRIPTURE

READ Judges 15:1-8 and **MARK** references to *Samson* and to *the Philistines.*

Judges 15:1-8

1 But after a while, in the time of wheat harvest, Samson visited his wife with a young goat, and said, "I will go in to my wife in her room." But her father did not let him enter.

2 Her father said, "I really thought that you hated her intensely; so I gave her to your companion. Is not her younger sister more beautiful than she? Please let her be yours instead."

3 Samson then said to them, "This time I shall be blameless in regard to the Philistines when I do them harm."

4 Samson went and caught three hundred foxes, and took torches, and turned the foxes tail to tail and put one torch in the middle between two tails.

5 When he had set fire to the torches, he released the foxes into the standing grain of the Philistines, thus burning up both the shocks and the standing grain, along with the vineyards and groves.

6 Then the Philistines said, "Who did this?" And they said, "Samson, the son-in-law of the Timnite, because he took his wife and gave her to his companion." So the Philistines came up and burned her and her father with fire.

7 Samson said to them, "Since you act like this, I will surely take revenge on you, but after that I will quit."

8 He struck them ruthlessly with a great slaughter; and he went down and lived in the cleft of the rock of Etam.

DISCUSS with your GROUP or PONDER on your own . . .

When does Samson finally return to Timnah for his wife? Describe his interaction with her father.

How does Samson react? How does he view his own behavior (verse 3)?

Do you ever rationalize negative behavior? If so, in what specific areas of your life do you tend to do this? How has that worked out for you? What would be a better approach?

How did it work out for Samson? What did the Philistines do in response? (Do you remember the threat they made to his wife during the wedding feast?)

After ruining their crops, what does Samson do to the Philistines according to verses 7 and 8? How does Samson describe his own behavior in verse 7?

What results have you seen firsthand as a result of revenge? What effect did it have on the vengeful party? What happened to the person on the receiving end?

Does revenge typically end or escalate a conflict? Why do you think that is?

Is there a situation in your life that you need to hand over to God instead of trying to exact revenge either through action or even through holding a grudge?

OBSERVE the TEXT of SCRIPTURE

READ Judges 15:9-20 and **MARK** references to *Samson* and *the men of Judah.*

Judges 15:9-20

9 Then the Philistines went up and camped in Judah, and spread out in Lehi.

10 The men of Judah said, "Why have you come up against us?" And they said, "We have come up to bind Samson in order to do to him as he did to us."

11 Then 3,000 men of Judah went down to the cleft of the rock of Etam and said to Samson, "Do you not know that the Philistines are rulers over us? What then is this that you have done to us?" And he said to them, "As they did to me, so I have done to them."

12 They said to him, "We have come down to bind you so that we may give you into the hands of the Philistines." And Samson said to them, "Swear to me that you will not kill me."

13 So they said to him, "No, but we will bind you fast and give you into their hands; yet surely we will not kill you." Then they bound him with two new ropes and brought him up from the rock.

14 When he came to Lehi, the Philistines shouted as they met him. And the Spirit of the LORD came upon him mightily so that the ropes that were on his arms were as flax that is burned with fire, and his bonds dropped from his hands.

15 He found a fresh jawbone of a donkey, so he reached out and took it and killed a thousand men with it.

16 Then Samson said, "With the jawbone of a donkey, Heaps upon heaps, With the jawbone of a donkey I have killed a thousand men."

17 When he had finished speaking, he threw the jawbone from his hand; and he named that place Ramath-lehi.

18 Then he became very thirsty, and he called to the LORD and said, "You have given this great deliverance by the hand of Your servant, and now shall I die of thirst and fall into the hands of the uncircumcised?"

19 But God split the hollow place that is in Lehi so that water came out of it. When he drank, his strength returned and he revived. Therefore he named it En-hakkore, which is in Lehi to this day.

20 So he judged Israel twenty years in the days of the Philistines.

DISCUSS with your GROUP or PONDER on your own . . .

Why do the Philistines come up against the men of Judah?

What do we learn about the men of Judah in this passage? What is their attitude toward the Philistines? Toward Samson?

What happens when Samson is given into the Philistine's hands?

How has the situation between Samson and the Philistines escalated step-by-step?

Is there anything you can learn from the combative behaviors of both Samson and the Philistines about how *not* to bring out the worst in people?

In the first recorded instance of Samson praying, what does he ask God for? How would you describe the tone of the prayer?

OBSERVE the TEXT of SCRIPTURE

READ Judges 16:1-17 and **MARK** references to *the lords of the Philistines* and to *Delilah*.

Judges 16:1-17

1 *Now Samson went to Gaza and saw a harlot there, and went in to her.*

2 When it was told *to the Gazites, saying, "Samson has come here,"* they surrounded the place *and lay in wait for him all night at the gate of the city. And they kept silent all night, saying, "Let us wait until the morning light, then we will kill him."*

3   Now Samson lay until midnight, and at midnight he arose and took hold of the doors of the city gate and the two posts and pulled them up along with the bars; then he put them on his shoulders and carried them up to the top of the mountain which is opposite Hebron.

4   After this it came about that he loved a woman in the valley of Sorek, whose name was Delilah.

5   The lords of the Philistines came up to her and said to her, "Entice him, and see where his great strength lies and how we may overpower him that we may bind him to afflict him. Then we will each give you eleven hundred pieces of silver."

6   So Delilah said to Samson, "Please tell me where your great strength is and how you may be bound to afflict you."

ONE STEP FURTHER:

Compare the Women

As you study this week, you will encounter many female characters: Samson's mother, his wife, a harlot, and Delilah. Compare these women with the women we've seen earlier in the book of Judges, including Achsah, Deborah, Jael, and the woman of Thebez. Record your observations below.

7 Samson said to her, "If they bind me with seven fresh cords that have not been dried, then I will become weak and be like any other man."

8 Then the lords of the Philistines brought up to her seven fresh cords that had not been dried, and she bound him with them.

9 Now she had men lying in wait in an inner room. And she said to him, "The Philistines are upon you, Samson!" But he snapped the cords as a string of tow snaps when it touches fire. So his strength was not discovered.

10 Then Delilah said to Samson, "Behold, you have deceived me and told me lies; now please tell me how you may be bound."

11 He said to her, "If they bind me tightly with new ropes which have not been used, then I will become weak and be like any other man."

12 So Delilah took new ropes and bound him with them and said to him, "The Philistines are upon you, Samson!" For the men were lying in wait in the inner room. But he snapped the ropes from his arms like a thread.

13 Then Delilah said to Samson, "Up to now you have deceived me and told me lies; tell me how you may be bound." And he said to her, "If you weave the seven locks of my hair with the web and fasten it with a pin, then I will become weak and be like any other man."

14 So while he slept, Delilah took the seven locks of his hair and wove them into the web. And she fastened it with the pin and said to him, "The Philistines are upon you, Samson!" But he awoke from his sleep and pulled out the pin of the loom and the web.

15 Then she said to him, "How can you say, 'I love you,' when your heart is not with me? You have deceived me these three times and have not told me where your great strength is."

16 It came about when she pressed him daily with her words and urged him, that his soul was annoyed to death.

17 So he told her all that was in his heart and said to her, "A razor has never come on my head, for I have been a Nazirite to God from my mother's womb. If I am shaved, then my strength will leave me and I will become weak and be like any other man."

DISCUSS with your GROUP or PONDER on your own . . .

Where is Samson as Judges 16 opens? Who is he with?

How do the people of the city think they will catch Samson? How does it turn out?

How has Samson measured up to the standards God gave the Israelites? What about His standards for a Nazarite?

Where does the scene shift to in verse 4? Who is the new main female character?

Describe Delilah from the text.

What do the lords of the Philistines ask her to do? What do they promise her? Does this sound familiar? If so, to what?

How does Delilah extract the secret of Samson's strength from him? Describe the process and what finally "works" on him.

OBSERVE the TEXT of SCRIPTURE

READ Judges 16:18-31 and **MARK** references to *Samson* and any references to his eyes.

Judges 16:18-31

18 *When Delilah saw that he had told her all that was in his heart, she sent and called the lords of the Philistines, saying, "Come up once more, for he has told me all that is in his heart." Then the lords of the Philistines came up to her and brought the money in their hands.*

19 *She made him sleep on her knees, and called for a man and had him shave off the seven locks of his hair. Then she began to afflict him, and his strength left him.*

20 *She said, "The Philistines are upon you, Samson!" And he awoke from his sleep and said, "I will go out as at other times and shake myself free." But he did not know that the LORD had departed from him.*

21 *Then the Philistines seized him and gouged out his eyes; and they brought him down to Gaza and bound him with bronze chains, and he was a grinder in the prison.*

22 *However, the hair of his head began to grow again after it was shaved off.*

23 *Now the lords of the Philistines assembled to offer a great sacrifice to Dagon their god, and to rejoice, for they said, "Our god has given Samson our enemy into our hands."*

24 *When the people saw him, they praised their god, for they said, "Our god has given our enemy into our hands, Even the destroyer of our country, Who has slain many of us."*

25 *It so happened when they were in high spirits, that they said, "Call for Samson, that he may amuse us." So they called for Samson from the prison, and he entertained them. And they made him stand between the pillars.*

26 *Then Samson said to the boy who was holding his hand, "Let me feel the pillars on which the house rests, that I may lean against them."*

27 *Now the house was full of men and women, and all the lords of the Philistines were there. And about 3,000 men and women were on the roof looking on while Samson was amusing them.*

28 *Then Samson called to the LORD and said, "O Lord GOD, please remember me and please strengthen me just this time, O God, that I may at once be avenged of the Philistines for my two eyes."*

29 *Samson grasped the two middle pillars on which the house rested, and braced himself against them, the one with his right hand and the other with his left.*

30 *And Samson said, "Let me die with the Philistines!" And he bent with all his might so that the house fell on the lords and all the people who were in it. So the dead whom he killed at his death were more than those whom he killed in his life.*

31 *Then his brothers and all his father's household came down, took him, brought him up and buried him between Zorah and Eshtaol in the tomb of Manoah his father. Thus he had judged Israel twenty years.*

DISCUSS with your GROUP or PONDER on your own . . .

What happens when the LORD departs from Samson? What do the Philistines do to him and for how long?

What opportunity does Samson have during a Philistine sacrifice? What does he ask God for and why?

What does Samson's request reveal about his heart?

How long does Samson judge Israel? Does he deliver the people thoroughly? Does the land have rest?

Think through the benefits Samson had in life. How well do you think he stewarded them?

How are you stewarding what God has entrusted to you?

@THE END OF THE DAY . . .

Go back to the final question and really take stock of it. What has God entrusted you with? What are your spiritual gifts? Your natural abilities? Where has God placed you specifically? Ask Him to show you how to follow Him fully starting right where you are today!

EXTRA
MEMORIZE | TWEET | POST | DRAW | HASHTAG | ENCODE | REMEMBER

Some more opportunities to review and remember!

Pick and Memorize a Key Verse for Each Chapter

Judges 13

Judges 14

Judges 15

Judges 16

"Tweet" It

Summarize the message of Judges 13 in 140 characters or less.

Summarize the message of Judges 14 in 140 characters or less.

Summarize the message of Judges 15 in 140 characters or less.

Summarize the message of Judges 16 in 140 characters or less.

#Hashtag It

Write a #hashtag for Judges 13.

#

Write a #hashtag for Judges 14.

#

Write a #hashtag for Judges 15.

#

Write a #hashtag for Judges 16.

#

From Bad to Worse to Unimaginable

In those days there was no king in Israel; every man did what was right in his own eyes.
—Judges 17:6

Just when you think it couldn't get any worse, the book of Judges records Israel's descent deeper and deeper into depravity! While the first 16 chapters have been largely silent about Israel's priests and Levites, the final chapters record incidents involving these "spiritual leaders." As you read, remember God doesn't sanction these actions that show in vivid detail the result of living contrary to His will and His ways.

REMEMBERING

Take some time to write down highlights from the first 16 chapters of Judges. Try to do this without looking back at your notes or previous chapters. Remember, just the highlights! (Take a cue from the amount of space you have!)

OBSERVE the TEXT of SCRIPTURE

READ Judges 17 and **MARK** every reference to *Micah*.

Judges 17

1　Now there was a man of the hill country of Ephraim whose name was Micah.

2　He said to his mother, "The eleven hundred pieces of silver which were taken from you, about which you uttered a curse in my hearing, behold, the silver is with me; I took it." And his mother said, "Blessed be my son by the LORD."

3　He then returned the eleven hundred pieces of silver to his mother, and his mother said, "I wholly dedicate the silver from my hand to the LORD for my son to make a graven image and a molten image; now therefore, I will return them to you."

4　So when he returned the silver to his mother, his mother took two hundred pieces of silver and gave them to the silversmith who made them into a graven image and a molten image, and they were in the house of Micah.

5　And the man Micah had a shrine and he made an ephod and household idols and consecrated one of his sons, that he might become his priest.

6　In those days there was no king in Israel; every man did what was right in his own eyes.

7　Now there was a young man from Bethlehem in Judah, of the family of Judah, who was a Levite; and he was staying there.

8 Then the man departed from the city, from Bethlehem in Judah, to stay wherever he might find a place; and as he made his journey, he came to the hill country of Ephraim to the house of Micah.

9 Micah said to him, "Where do you come from?" And he said to him, "I am a Levite from Bethlehem in Judah, and I am going to stay wherever I may find a place."

10 Micah then said to him, "Dwell with me and be a father and a priest to me, and I will give you ten pieces of silver a year, a suit of clothes, and your maintenance." So the Levite went in.

11 The Levite agreed to live with the man, and the young man became to him like one of his sons.

12 So Micah consecrated the Levite, and the young man became his priest and lived in the house of Micah.

13 Then Micah said, "Now I know that the LORD will prosper me, seeing I have a Levite as priest."

DISCUSS with your GROUP or PONDER on your own . . .

What thoughts were going through your head as you read this passage? Go ahead and write down any initial responses, reactions, or questions.

What in this passage might be rationalized as "right" or at least have some "God-sounding" veneer?

What obvious problems with the people's behavior are in this passage?

Whenever I'm faced with a passage (or life situation!) that is confusing or unclear, I start by asking "What *is* clear?" *Is anything clearly wrong? Is anything undeniably right? Are people acting in accordance with the revealed will of God or are they twisting things to their own liking?* In this case, let's hold up Micah and his mother's behavior to the simple and clear teaching of the Ten Commandments, which are printed on the following page for quick reference

Micah's Actions	God's Clear Teaching

Micah's Mama's Actions	God's Clear Teaching

The Ten Commandments (Exodus 20:3-17)

1. *"You shall have no other gods before Me."*

2. *"You shall not make for yourself an idol, or any likeness of what is in heaven above or on the earth beneath or in the water under the earth. You shall not worship them or serve them; for I, the LORD your God, am a jealous God, visiting the iniquity of the fathers on the children, on the third and the fourth generations of those who hate Me, but showing lovingkindness to thousands, to those who love Me and keep My commandments."*

3. *"You shall not take the name of the LORD your God in vain, for the LORD will not leave him unpunished who takes His name in vain."*

4. *"Remember the sabbath day, to keep it holy. Six days you shall labor and do all your work, but the seventh day is a sabbath of the LORD your God; in it you shall not do any work, you or your son or your daughter, your male or your female servant or your cattle or your sojourner who stays with you. For in six days the LORD made the heavens and the earth, the sea and all that is in them, and rested on the seventh day; therefore the LORD blessed the sabbath day and made it holy."*

5. *"Honor your father and your mother, that your days may be prolonged in the land which the LORD your God gives you."*

6. *"You shall not murder."*

7. *"You shall not commit adultery."*

8. *"You shall not steal."*

9. *"You shall not bear false witness against your neighbor."*

10. *"You shall not covet your neighbor's house; you shall not covet your neighbor's wife or his male servant or his female servant or his ox or his donkey or anything that belongs to your neighbor."*

DIGGING DEEPER
What's Wrong with the Levite?

Take some time this week to closely consider the Levite in this account by studying for yourself what the Bible teaches about Levites.

Start by using a concordance to identify where the term "Levite" appears in the Bible from Genesis through Judges and how it's used. List the highlights of what you learn below.

Next, do the same with the term "priest" in the same books.

Based on what you've learned, how *should* the Levite have responded to Micah's job offer? What *should* he have been doing?

How do you think the condition of the people correlated with the condition of the Levites? Do you think similar correlations exist in the Church today? Explain.

What benefit did Micah think having a Levite as a priest would bring him? What does this show us about his view of God?

Have you thought you could manipulate God, to force His hand? Explain. What does this reveal about *your* view of God?

How does a person's view of God affect his day-to-day behavior? How does it affect yours?

OBSERVE the TEXT of SCRIPTURE

READ Judges 18:1-7 and **MARK** references to the *five men* and to the *Levite*.

Judges 18:1-7

1 *In those days there was no king of Israel; and in those days the tribe of the Danites was seeking an inheritance for themselves to live in, for until that day an inheritance had not been allotted to them as a possession among the tribes of Israel.*

2 *So the sons of Dan sent from their family five men out of their whole number, valiant men from Zorah and Eshtaol, to spy out the land and to search it; and they said to them, "Go, search the land." And they came to the hill country of Ephraim, to the house of Micah, and lodged there.*

3 When they were near the house of Micah, they recognized the voice of the young man, the Levite; and they turned aside there and said to him, "Who brought you here? And what are you doing in this place? And what do you have here?"

4 He said to them, "Thus and so has Micah done to me, and he has hired me and I have become his priest."

5 They said to him, "Inquire of God, please, that we may know whether our way on which we are going will be prosperous."

6 The priest said to them, "Go in peace; your way in which you are going has the LORD'S approval."

7 Then the five men departed and came to Laish and saw the people who were in it living in security, after the manner of the Sidonians, quiet and secure; for there was no ruler humiliating them for anything in the land, and they were far from the Sidonians and had no dealings with anyone.

DISCUSS with your GROUP or PONDER on your own . . .

What familiar phrase does the chapter begin with? What familiar spiritual condition does this lead to?

Why were the Danites looking for a place to live?

How does this account compare with what Joshua 19:40-48 reports? What land were they supposed to take as a possession?

Do any of these places in Joshua 19:40-48 ring a bell? Where have we read about them before?

Do you think it was right for the people to go after this other land when God had already allotted a specific inheritance for them? Why/why not?

Do we sometimes pass off our ideas as God-approved? If so, how? What do you think typically prompts this?

What did you learn about the five men in Judges 18? (Who were they? What were they doing? Where were they going? Who did they meet along the way?)

Describe the interaction between the Levite and the five men from Dan. (Did they view his priesthood as legitimate? Explain. What do the five men find on their mission?)

OBSERVE the TEXT of SCRIPTURE

READ Judges 18:8-31 and continue to **MARK** references to the *five men*, to the *Levite.* Also **MARK** references to *Micah.*

Judges 18:8-31

8　When they came back to their brothers at Zorah and Eshtaol, their brothers said to them, "What do you report?"

9　They said, "Arise, and let us go up against them; for we have seen the land, and behold, it is very good. And will you sit still? Do not delay to go, to enter, to possess the land.

10　"When you enter, you will come to a secure people with a spacious land; for God has given it into your hand, a place where there is no lack of anything that is on the earth."

11　Then from the family of the Danites, from Zorah and from Eshtaol, six hundred men armed with weapons of war set out.

12　They went up and camped at Kiriath-jearim in Judah. Therefore they called that place Mahaneh-dan to this day; behold, it is west of Kiriath-jearim.

13　They passed from there to the hill country of Ephraim and came to the house of Micah.

14　Then the five men who went to spy out the country of Laish said to their kinsmen, "Do you know that there are in these houses an ephod and household idols and a graven image and a molten image? Now therefore, consider what you should do."

15　They turned aside there and came to the house of the young man, the Levite, to the house of Micah, and asked him of his welfare.

16　The six hundred men armed with their weapons of war, who were of the sons of Dan, stood by the entrance of the gate.

17　Now the five men who went to spy out the land went up and entered there, and took the graven image and the ephod and household idols and the molten image, while the priest stood by the entrance of the gate with the six hundred men armed with weapons of war.

18　When these went into Micah's house and took the graven image, the ephod and household idols and the molten image, the priest said to them, "What are you doing?"

19　They said to him, "Be silent, put your hand over your mouth and come with us, and be to us a father and a priest. Is it better for you to be a priest to the house of one man, or to be priest to a tribe and a family in Israel?"

20 The priest's heart was glad, and he took the ephod and household idols and the graven image and went among the people.

21 Then they turned and departed, and put the little ones and the livestock and the valuables in front of them.

22 When they had gone some distance from the house of Micah, the men who were in the houses near Micah's house assembled and overtook the sons of Dan.

23 They cried to the sons of Dan, who turned around and said to Micah, "What is the matter with you, that you have assembled together?"

24 He said, "You have taken away my gods which I made, and the priest, and have gone away, and what do I have besides? So how can you say to me, 'What is the matter with you?' "

25 The sons of Dan said to him, "Do not let your voice be heard among us, or else fierce men will fall upon you and you will lose your life, with the lives of your household."

26 So the sons of Dan went on their way; and when Micah saw that they were too strong for him, he turned and went back to his house.

27 Then they took what Micah had made and the priest who had belonged to him, and came to Laish, to a people quiet and secure, and struck them with the edge of the sword; and they burned the city with fire.

28 And there was no one to deliver them, because it was far from Sidon and they had no dealings with anyone, and it was in the valley which is near Beth-rehob. And they rebuilt the city and lived in it.

29 They called the name of the city Dan, after the name of Dan their father who was born in Israel; however, the name of the city formerly was Laish.

30 The sons of Dan set up for themselves the graven image; and Jonathan, the son of Gershom, the son of Manasseh, he and his sons were priests to the tribe of the Danites until the day of the captivity of the land.

31 So they set up for themselves Micah's graven image which he had made, all the time that the house of God was at Shiloh.

DISCUSS with your GROUP or PONDER on your own . . .

What report do the five men bring back to the rest of the tribe of Dan?

Who do they bring on their second trip? What do they say about the house of Micah? What happens when they stop there the second time?

How does the priest respond? What does he do? What do you think he is ultimately trusting in? Why?

How does Micah react when he hears the news? What is *he* trusting?

Do you trust things that have a godly veneer but no true substance? What are some examples and why do you trust them?

How does a person or people move from trusting in God to trusting in idols? What steps along the path do you see from this story?

What steps tempt you in similar directions today?

According to Judges 18:30, who served as the Danites' priests?
Compare Judges 18:30 in the NASB and ESV translations in the FYI box
below.

How long does the idolatry last?

Based on the last verse (31), where were the people supposed to
worship?

**:**

Two Translations of Judges 18:30

The addition of one letter *(nun)* to a version of the Hebrew Scriptures called the Masoretic Text—
copied and edited between the 7th and 10th centuries AD—accounts for the difference between the
ESV's "Moses" and the NASB's "Manasseh."

ESV

*And the people of Dan set up the carved image for themselves, and Jonathan the son of Gershom,
son of Moses, and his sons were priests to the tribe of the Danites until the day of the captivity of
the land.*

NASB

*The sons of Dan set up for themselves the graven image; and Jonathan, the son of Gershom, the
son of Manasseh, he and his sons were priests to the tribe of the Danites until the day of the captivity of the land.*

The Grandson of Moses

If the Levite was, in fact, Moses' grandson as the text seems to indicate, this supports the view that the final section of Judges occurred toward the beginning of the period of the judges.

What do you know about how God wants us to worship today? Can you find Scripture references? Do you think this is important? Explain.

OBSERVE the TEXT of SCRIPTURE

READ Judges 19:1-10 and **MARK** references to the *Levite*, his *concubine*, and her *father*. Remember to include synonyms and pronouns.

Judges 19:1-10

1 Now it came about in those days, when there was no king in Israel, that there was a certain Levite staying in the remote part of the hill country of Ephraim, who took a concubine for himself from Bethlehem in Judah.

2 But his concubine played the harlot against him, and she went away from him to her father's house in Bethlehem in Judah, and was there for a period of four months.

3 Then her husband arose and went after her to speak tenderly to her in order to bring her back, taking with him his servant and a pair of donkeys. So she brought him into her father's house, and when the girl's father saw him, he was glad to meet him.

4 His father-in-law, the girl's father, detained him; and he remained with him three days. So they ate and drank and lodged there.

5 Now on the fourth day they got up early in the morning, and he prepared to go; and the girl's father said to his son-in-law, "Sustain yourself with a piece of bread, and afterward you may go."

6 So both of them sat down and ate and drank together; and the girl's father said to the man, "Please be willing to spend the night, and let your heart be merry."

7 *Then the man arose to go, but his father-in-law urged him so that he spent the night there again.*

8 *On the fifth day he arose to go early in the morning, and the girl's father said, "Please sustain yourself, and wait until afternoon"; so both of them ate.*

9 *When the man arose to go along with his concubine and servant, his father-in-law, the girl's father, said to him, "Behold now, the day has drawn to a close; please spend the night. Lo, the day is coming to an end; spend the night here that your heart may be merry. Then tomorrow you may arise early for your journey so that you may go home."*

10 *But the man was not willing to spend the night, so he arose and departed and came to a place opposite Jebus (that is, Jerusalem). And there were with him a pair of saddled donkeys; his concubine also was with him.*

DISCUSS with your GROUP or PONDER on your own . . .

What questions do you have after reading Judges 19:1-10? Does anything in the situation seem "not quite right"?

What repeated phrase begins this chapter? Again, what does this signal to the reader?

Who is the main character in this section? Describe his situation.

How long does it take for the Levite to act?

What happens when he arrives at the father's house? Describe the hospitality shown him.

OBSERVE the TEXT of SCRIPTURE

READ Judges 19:11-25 and **MARK** references to *Gibeah* and *the men* of Gibeah. Remember to include synonyms and pronouns.

Judges 19:11-25

11 *When they were near Jebus, the day was almost gone; and the servant said to his master, "Please come, and let us turn aside into this city of the Jebusites and spend the night in it."*

12 *However, his master said to him, "We will not turn aside into the city of foreigners who are not of the sons of Israel; but we will go on as far as Gibeah."*

13 *He said to his servant, "Come and let us approach one of these places; and we will spend the night in Gibeah or Ramah."*

14 *So they passed along and went their way, and the sun set on them near Gibeah which belongs to Benjamin.*

15 *They turned aside there in order to enter and lodge in Gibeah. When they entered, they sat down in the open square of the city, for no one took them into his house to spend the night.*

16 *Then behold, an old man was coming out of the field from his work at evening. Now the man was from the hill country of Ephraim, and he was staying in Gibeah, but the men of the place were Benjamites.*

17 And he lifted up his eyes and saw the traveler in the open square of
    the city; and the old man said, "Where are you going, and where
    do you come from?"

18 He said to him, "We are passing from Bethlehem in Judah to the
    remote part of the hill country of Ephraim, for I am from there, and
    I went to Bethlehem in Judah. But I am now going to my house,
    and no man will take me into his house.

19 "Yet there is both straw and fodder for our donkeys, and also bread
    and wine for me, your maidservant, and the young man who is
    with your servants; there is no lack of anything."

20 The old man said, "Peace to you. Only let me take care of all your
    needs; however, do not spend the night in the open square."

21 So he took him into his house and gave the donkeys fodder, and
    they washed their feet and ate and drank.

22 While they were celebrating, behold, the men of the city, certain
    worthless fellows, surrounded the house, pounding the door; and
    they spoke to the owner of the house, the old man, saying, "Bring
    out the man who came into your house that we may have relations
    with him."

23 Then the man, the owner of the house, went out to them and said
    to them, "No, my fellows, please do not act so wickedly; since this
    man has come into my house, do not commit this act of folly.

24 "Here is my virgin daughter and his concubine. Please let me bring
    them out that you may ravish them and do to them whatever you
    wish. But do not commit such an act of folly against this man."

25 But the men would not listen to him. So the man seized his
    concubine and brought her out to them; and they raped her and
    abused her all night until morning, then let her go at the approach
    of dawn.

DISCUSS with your GROUP or PONDER on your own . . .

Who is in the traveling party? Why do they decide to stop in Gibeah?

What initial options do they have for lodging as night falls? What do they decide and why?

Who eventually offers hospitality to the travelers? What does he do for them?

Describe the men who surround the house. Who are they and what do they do?

How do the old man and the Levite respond to the threat? What do you think would have been an appropriate response?

What happens?

How does this whole encounter differ from the hospitality shown to the Levite by his father-in-law?

OBSERVE the TEXT of SCRIPTURE

READ Judges 19:26-30 and **MARK** references to *the woman* and *her master*. Remember to include synonyms and pronouns. Also **MARK** all references to the time of day.

Judges 19:26-30

26 As the day began to dawn, the woman came and fell down at the doorway of the man's house where her master was, until full daylight.

27 When her master arose in the morning and opened the doors of the house and went out to go on his way, then behold, his concubine was lying at the doorway of the house with her hands on the threshold.

28 He said to her, "Get up and let us go," but there was no answer. Then he placed her on the donkey; and the man arose and went to his home.

29 When he entered his house, he took a knife and laid hold of his concubine and cut her in twelve pieces, limb by limb, and sent her throughout the territory of Israel.

ONE STEP FURTHER:

Think Through the Connections

Spend some time this week thinking broadly of other connections in Scripture. Do you recall any other accounts of men demanding that strangers be given to them to violate? How does this kind of behavior reflect on society as a whole? Can you think of any scriptural cross-references that comment on this kind of behavior? (Hint: Some of the cross-references that come to mind for me are in Genesis and Romans.)

30 *All who saw* it *said, "Nothing like this has ever happened or been seen from the day when the sons of Israel came up from the land of Egypt to this day. Consider it, take counsel and speak up!"*

DISCUSS with your GROUP or PONDER on your own . . .

What time references did you mark? What happened at each time?

How does the Levite's relationship to the woman change in this section? Compare it with the relationship mentioned in verse 3.

If you knew a person was being brutalized outside of your house, how would it affect you emotionally? Would you be able to relax? To sleep?

Now, having considered this, compare how the Levite behaves. What happens in the morning? Does this reveal anything about him?

What does the text say specifically about the woman? What is her condition? Do you think she is dead? Why/why not?

What does the Levite do when he gets back home? Why do you think he does it?

How is he perceived by those who saw? What do they say about it?

OBSERVE the TEXT of SCRIPTURE

READ Judges 20:1-7 and again **MARK** references to *Gibeah*.

Judges 20:1-7

1   Then all the sons of Israel from Dan to Beersheba, including the land of Gilead, came out, and the congregation assembled as one man to the LORD at Mizpah.

2   The chiefs of all the people, even of all the tribes of Israel, took their stand in the assembly of the people of God, 400,000 foot soldiers who drew the sword.

3   (Now the sons of Benjamin heard that the sons of Israel had gone up to Mizpah.) And the sons of Israel said, "Tell us, how did this wickedness take place?"

4   So the Levite, the husband of the woman who was murdered, answered and said, "I came with my concubine to spend the night at Gibeah which belongs to Benjamin.

5 "But the men of Gibeah rose up against me and surrounded the house at night because of me. They intended to kill me; instead, they ravished my concubine so that she died.

6 "And I took hold of my concubine and cut her in pieces and sent her throughout the land of Israel's inheritance; for they have committed a lewd and disgraceful act in Israel.

7 "Behold, all you sons of Israel, give your advice and counsel here."

DISCUSS with your GROUP or PONDER on your own . . .

Where and why do the people assemble together? What tribe is absent?

How does the Levite describe the events that took place at Gibeah?

If you had only heard his account, what would you think of the situation? Of him?

Compare the Levite's account with Judges 19. What does he leave out? What does he add?

Dan to Beersheba

The phrase "Dan to Beersheba" includes the northernmost part of Israel (Dan) and the southern-most (Beersheba), all Israel from north to south.

Are the men of Gibeah the only ones who have committed the "lewd and disgraceful" act? Explain your answer.

Whose counsel does the Levite seek? Where should he be seeking it?

OBSERVE the TEXT of SCRIPTURE

READ Judges 20:8-13 and **MARK** references to the tribe and people of *Benjamin*.

Judges 20:8-13

8 *Then all the people arose as one man, saying, "Not one of us will go to his tent, nor will any of us return to his house.*

9 *"But now this is the thing which we will do to Gibeah; we will go up against it by lot.*

10 *"And we will take 10 men out of 100 throughout the tribes of Israel, and 100 out of 1,000, and 1,000 out of 10,000 to supply food for the people, that when they come to Gibeah of Benjamin, they may punish them for all the disgraceful acts that they have committed in Israel."*

11 *Thus all the men of Israel were gathered against the city, united as one man.*

12 *Then the tribes of Israel sent men through the entire tribe of Benjamin, saying, "What is this wickedness that has taken place among you?*

13 *"Now then, deliver up the men, the worthless fellows in Gibeah, that we may put them to death and remove this wickedness from Israel." But the sons of Benjamin would not listen to the voice of their brothers, the sons of Israel.*

DISCUSS with your GROUP or PONDER on your own . . .

What course of action do the sons of Israel choose and for what purpose? How do they decide?

For the record, what has been going on among the other tribes of Israel? How are they living? Are they using a reliable moral compass?

Let's take a moment here. Do you ever chart a course based on the lives of others around you as opposed to on God's revealed truth? In what ways can this pose a temptation in your life?

What happens when the sons of Israel ask the Benjamites to hand over the "worthless fellows" from Gibeah?

OBSERVE the TEXT of SCRIPTURE

READ Judges 20:14-48 and again MARK references to the tribe and people of Benjamin.

Judges 20:14-48

14 The sons of Benjamin gathered from the cities to Gibeah, to go out to battle against the sons of Israel.

15 From the cities on that day the sons of Benjamin were numbered, 26,000 men who draw the sword, besides the inhabitants of Gibeah who were numbered, 700 choice men.

16 Out of all these people 700 choice men were left-handed; each one could sling a stone at a hair and not miss.

17 Then the men of Israel besides Benjamin were numbered, 400,000 men who draw the sword; all these were men of war.

18 Now the sons of Israel arose, went up to Bethel, and inquired of God and said, "Who shall go up first for us to battle against the sons of Benjamin?" Then the LORD said, "Judah shall go up first."

19 So the sons of Israel arose in the morning and camped against Gibeah.

20 The men of Israel went out to battle against Benjamin, and the men of Israel arrayed for battle against them at Gibeah.

21 Then the sons of Benjamin came out of Gibeah and felled to the ground on that day 22,000 men of Israel.

22 But the people, the men of Israel, encouraged themselves and arrayed for battle again in the place where they had arrayed themselves the first day.

23 The sons of Israel went up and wept before the LORD until evening, and inquired of the LORD, saying, "Shall we again draw near for battle against the sons of my brother Benjamin?" And the LORD said, "Go up against him."

24 Then the sons of Israel came against the sons of Benjamin the second day.

25 Benjamin went out against them from Gibeah the second day and felled to the ground again 18,000 men of the sons of Israel; all these drew the sword.

26 Then all the sons of Israel and all the people went up and came to Bethel and wept; thus they remained there before the LORD and fasted that day until evening. And they offered burnt offerings and peace offerings before the LORD.

27 The sons of Israel inquired of the LORD (for the ark of the covenant of God was there in those days,

28 and Phinehas the son of Eleazar, Aaron's son, stood before it to minister *in those days*), *saying, "Shall I yet again go out to battle against the sons of my brother Benjamin, or shall I cease?" And the LORD said, "Go up, for tomorrow I will deliver them into your hand."*

29 *So Israel set men in ambush around Gibeah.*

30 *The sons of Israel went up against the sons of Benjamin on the third day and arrayed themselves against Gibeah as at other times.*

31 *The sons of Benjamin went out against the people and were drawn away from the city, and they began to strike and kill some of the people as at other times, on the highways, one of which goes up to Bethel and the other to Gibeah,* and *in the field, about thirty men of Israel.*

32 *The sons of Benjamin said, "They are struck down before us, as at the first." But the sons of Israel said, "Let us flee that we may draw them away from the city to the highways."*

33 *Then all the men of Israel arose from their place and arrayed themselves at Baal-tamar; and the men of Israel in ambush broke out of their place, even out of Maareh-geba.*

34 *When ten thousand choice men from all Israel came against Gibeah, the battle became fierce; but Benjamin did not know that disaster was close to them.*

35 *And the LORD struck Benjamin before Israel, so that the sons of Israel destroyed 25,100 men of Benjamin that day, all who draw the sword.*

ONE STEP FURTHER:

One Bright Spot

In an overwhelmingly dark time, Phinehas the grandson of Aaron, stands out as a light. If you have time this week, see what else he is remembered for in the pages of Scripture. Record your findings below.

36 So the sons of Benjamin saw that they were defeated. When the men of Israel gave ground to Benjamin because they relied on the men in ambush whom they had set against Gibeah,

37 the men in ambush hurried and rushed against Gibeah; the men in ambush also deployed and struck all the city with the edge of the sword.

38 Now the appointed sign between the men of Israel and the men in ambush was that they would make a great cloud of smoke rise from the city.

39 Then the men of Israel turned in the battle, and Benjamin began to strike and kill about thirty men of Israel, for they said, "Surely they are defeated before us, as in the first battle."

40 But when the cloud began to rise from the city in a column of smoke, Benjamin looked behind them; and behold, the whole city was going up in smoke to heaven.

41 Then the men of Israel turned, and the men of Benjamin were terrified; for they saw that disaster was close to them.

42 Therefore, they turned their backs before the men of Israel toward the direction of the wilderness, but the battle overtook them while those who came out of the cities destroyed them in the midst of them.

43 They surrounded Benjamin, pursued them without rest and trod them down opposite Gibeah toward the east.

44 Thus 18,000 men of Benjamin fell; all these were valiant warriors.

45 The rest turned and fled toward the wilderness to the rock of Rimmon, but they caught 5,000 of them on the highways and overtook them at Gidom and killed 2,000 of them.

46 So all of Benjamin who fell that day were 25,000 men who draw the sword; all these were valiant warriors.

47 But 600 men turned and fled toward the wilderness to the rock of Rimmon, and they remained at the rock of Rimmon four months.

48 The men of Israel then turned back against the sons of Benjamin and struck them with the edge of the sword, both the entire city with the cattle and all that they found; they also set on fire all the cities which they found.

DISCUSS with your GROUP or PONDER on your own . . .

How many Benjamites gather to Gibeah to fight against the rest of Israel?

Describe their fighting men.

What role does God play in all of this? What does Israel want to know from Him and when do they ask?

Who would you say devised the plan of attack? Explain your answer from the text.

Describe what happens in the battle on each day and how the people respond.

	Battle Results	Israel's Response
Day One		
Day Two		
Day Three		

What changes in Israel's interactions with the LORD as the battle lingers on? How does the battle resolve?

Finally, compare verse 18 with Judges 1. How have things changed?

OBSERVE the TEXT of SCRIPTURE

READ Judges 21:1-15 and **MARK** every occurrence of *Jabesh-gilead*.

Judges 21:1-15

1 Now the men of Israel had sworn in Mizpah, saying, "None of us shall give his daughter to Benjamin in marriage."

2 So the people came to Bethel and sat there before God until evening, and lifted up their voices and wept bitterly.

3 They said, "Why, O LORD, God of Israel, has this come about in Israel, so that one tribe should be missing today in Israel?"

4 It came about the next day that the people arose early and built an altar there and offered burnt offerings and peace offerings.

5 Then the sons of Israel said, "Who is there among all the tribes of Israel who did not come up in the assembly to the LORD?" For they had taken a great oath concerning him who did not come up to the LORD at Mizpah, saying, "He shall surely be put to death."

6 And the sons of Israel were sorry for their brother Benjamin and said, "One tribe is cut off from Israel today.

7 "What shall we do for wives for those who are left, since we have sworn by the LORD not to give them any of our daughters in marriage?"

8 And they said, "What one is there of the tribes of Israel who did not come up to the LORD at Mizpah?" And behold, no one had come to the camp from Jabesh-gilead to the assembly.

9 For when the people were numbered, behold, not one of the inhabitants of Jabesh-gilead was there.

10 *And the congregation sent 12,000 of the valiant warriors there, and commanded them, saying, "Go and strike the inhabitants of Jabesh-gilead with the edge of the sword, with the women and the little ones.*

11 *"This is the thing that you shall do: you shall utterly destroy every man and every woman who has lain with a man."*

12 *And they found among the inhabitants of Jabesh-gilead 400 young virgins who had not known a man by lying with him; and they brought them to the camp at Shiloh, which is in the land of Canaan.*

13 *Then the whole congregation sent word and spoke to the sons of Benjamin who were at the rock of Rimmon, and proclaimed peace to them.*

14 *Benjamin returned at that time, and they gave them the women whom they had kept alive from the women of Jabesh-gilead; yet they were not enough for them.*

15 *And the people were sorry for Benjamin because the LORD had made a breach in the tribes of Israel.*

DISCUSS with your GROUP or PONDER on your own . . .

What unwise vow do the people lament at the beginning of Judges 21?

What do the people ask the LORD in verse 3? Based on Scripture, how would you answer the question?

How do they set about to solve the problem at hand? Any thoughts about what their first step should have been?

What does the text say about Jabesh-gilead?

How does what happened to the people of Jabesh-gilead compare to other injustices we've seen in this account?

OBSERVE the TEXT of SCRIPTURE

READ Judges 21:16-25 and **MARK** every occurrence of *daughters of Shiloh*.

Judges 21:16-25

16 Then the elders of the congregation said, "What shall we do for wives for those who are left, since the women are destroyed out of Benjamin?"

17 They said, "There must be an inheritance for the survivors of Benjamin, so that a tribe will not be blotted out from Israel.

18 "But we cannot give them wives of our daughters." For the sons of Israel had sworn, saying, "Cursed is he who gives a wife to Benjamin."

19 So they said, "Behold, there is a feast of the LORD from year to year in Shiloh, which is on the north side of Bethel, on the east side of the highway that goes up from Bethel to Shechem, and on the south side of Lebonah."

20 And they commanded the sons of Benjamin, saying, "Go and lie in wait in the vineyards,

21 and watch; and behold, if the daughters of Shiloh come out to take part in the dances, then you shall come out of the vineyards and each of you shall catch his wife from the daughters of Shiloh, and go to the land of Benjamin.

22 "It shall come about, when their fathers or their brothers come to complain to us, that we shall say to them, 'Give them to us voluntarily, because we did not take for each man of Benjamin a wife in battle, nor did you give them to them, else you would now be guilty.' "

23 The sons of Benjamin did so, and took wives according to their number from those who danced, whom they carried away. And they went and returned to their inheritance and rebuilt the cities and lived in them.

24 The sons of Israel departed from there at that time, every man to his tribe and family, and each one of them went out from there to his inheritance.

25 In those days there was no king in Israel; everyone did what was right in his own eyes.

DISCUSS with your GROUP or PONDER on your own . . .

What remaining problem do the sons of Israel have after the women of Jabesh-gilead are given to Benjamin?

How do they solve the problem this time?

Looking back through Judges 20 and 21, how many people have been affected by the incident at Gibeah and in what ways? You might want to start with the daughters of Shiloh.

How did doing what was right in their own eyes work for Israel?

How has doing what is right in your own eyes worked for you?

What ways have you seen sin—your own or the sin of others—spread and/or affect people?

@THE END OF THE DAY . . .

As we come to the end of Judges, take some time to review what we've learned and ask God to cement key truths to your heart. Don't write anything down yet. Think through them, pray through them, and then write down the key applications you want to be able to remember next year!

The book of Judges starts with great hope as the children of Israel enter the promised land, but it ends desperately hopeless as the people continually wander back into sin. Human deliverers, after all, can only do so much.

As we wrap up next week, we'll look at one final account that comes to us from the time of the judges—the story of a Moabite woman named Ruth through whose line the one true Deliverer would eventually come!

EXTRA
MEMORIZE | TWEET | POST | DRAW | HASHTAG | ENCODE | REMEMBER

Some more opportunities to review and remember!

Pick and Memorize a Key Verse for Each Chapter

Judges 17

Judges 18

Judges 19

Judges 20

Judges 21

"Tweet" It

Summarize the message of Judges 17 in 140 characters or less.

Summarize the message of Judges 18 in 140 characters or less.

Summarize the message of Judges 19 in 140 characters or less.

Summarize the message of Judges 20 in 140 characters or less.

Summarize the message of Judges 21 in 140 characters or less.

#Hashtag It

Write a #hashtag for Judges 17.

#

Write a #hashtag for Judges 18.

#

Write a #hashtag for Judges 19.

#

Write a #hashtag for Judges 20.

#

Write a #hashtag for Judges 21.

#

Future Hope

Salmon was the father of Boaz by Rahab,
Boaz was the father of Obed by Ruth,
and Obed the father of Jesse.
Jesse was the father of David the king.
—Matthew 1:5-6a

From all you've learned so far, how depressing would it be to end a study of Judges at the end of Judges? There are so many lessons for sure—people wander and rebel against God, God judges sin, He delivers when people cry out to Him—but the picture of defeat and sin cycles that Judges paints is both frightening and disturbing. Judges shows the bad news of the human condition in all its fallen detail.

The time of the judges, though, was not without hope. While the people cycled deeper and deeper into sin, God was paving the way for Israel's—and the world's—one true Deliverer, an Israelite king descended from, among others, a God-fearing Moabite woman!

REMEMBERING

Briefly summarize what you learned about the moral climate of Israel during the time of the judges.

Flash-Forward to Matthew

As we begin today with a few verses from Matthew's Gospel we'll set the scene for our final lesson by looking at the larger biblical landscape. Matthew, who wrote to a Jewish audience, over and over again shows Jesus fulfilling Old Testament prophecy.

OBSERVE the TEXT of SCRIPTURE

READ Matthew 1:1-6, 16-17 and **UNDERLINE** references to each of Jesus' male ancestors. **CIRCLE** references to each of His female ancestors.

Matthew 1:1–6, 16-17

1   The record of the genealogy of Jesus the Messiah, the son of David, the son of Abraham:

2   Abraham was the father of Isaac, Isaac the father of Jacob, and Jacob the father of Judah and his brothers.

3   Judah was the father of Perez and Zerah by Tamar, Perez was the father of Hezron, and Hezron the father of Ram.

4   Ram was the father of Amminadab, Amminadab the father of Nahshon, and Nahshon the father of Salmon.

5   Salmon was the father of Boaz by Rahab, Boaz was the father of Obed by Ruth, and Obed the father of Jesse.

6   Jesse was the father of David the king. David was the father of Solomon by Bathsheba who had been the wife of Uriah.

16   Jacob was the father of Joseph the husband of Mary, by whom Jesus was born, who is called the Messiah.

17 *So all the generations from Abraham to David are fourteen
generations; from David to the deportation to Babylon, fourteen
generations; and from the deportation to Babylon to the Messiah,
fourteen generations.*

DISCUSS with your GROUP or PONDER on your own . . .

How does Matthew describe Jesus in verse 1?

List Jesus' male ancestors mentioned in Matthew 1:1-6.

Which of Jesus' female ancestors does Matthew record?

Which names from the geneaology do you recognize? Briefly note what
you know about them.

Son of David, Son of Abraham

By calling Jesus "the son of David" and "the son of Abraham," Matthew asserts that Jesus fulfills
two major Old Testament prophecies (see Genesis 12 and 2 Samuel 7).

Back to the Time of the Judges

As we settle back into the judges' era with the book of Ruth, we will have to leave some stones unturned for the sake of time.

OBSERVE the TEXT of SCRIPTURE

READ Ruth 1 and **MARK** the word *return* (also *gone back* and *turn back*).

Ruth 1

1   Now it came about in the days when the judges governed, that there was a famine in the land. And a certain man of Bethlehem in Judah went to sojourn in the land of Moab with his wife and his two sons.

2   The name of the man was Elimelech, and the name of his wife, Naomi; and the names of his two sons were Mahlon and Chilion, Ephrathites of Bethlehem in Judah. Now they entered the land of Moab and remained there.

3   Then Elimelech, Naomi's husband, died; and she was left with her two sons.

4   They took for themselves Moabite women as wives; the name of the one was Orpah and the name of the other Ruth. And they lived there about ten years.

5   Then both Mahlon and Chilion also died, and the woman was bereft of her two children and her husband.

6   Then she arose with her daughters-in-law that she might return from the land of Moab, for she had heard in the land of Moab that the LORD had visited His people in giving them food.

7   So she departed from the place where she was, and her two daughters-in-law with her; and they went on the way to return to the land of Judah.

8   And Naomi said to her two daughters-in-law, "Go, return each of you to her mother's house. May the LORD deal kindly with you as you have dealt with the dead and with me.

9   "May the LORD grant that you may find rest, each in the house of her husband." Then she kissed them, and they lifted up their voices and wept.

What is a Moabite?

If you have extra time this week see what you can learn about Ruth's ancestors, the Moabites. Using a concordance, search on the term "Moab*" and see what you discover. Record your findings below.

10 And they said to her, "No, but we will surely return with you to your people."

11 But Naomi said, "Return, my daughters. Why should you go with me? Have I yet sons in my womb, that they may be your husbands?

12 "Return, my daughters! Go, for I am too old to have a husband. If I said I have hope, if I should even have a husband tonight and also bear sons,

13 would you therefore wait until they were grown? Would you therefore refrain from marrying? No, my daughters; for it is harder for me than for you, for the hand of the LORD has gone forth against me."

14 And they lifted up their voices and wept again; and Orpah kissed her mother-in-law, but Ruth clung to her.

15 Then she said, "Behold, your sister-in-law has gone back to her people and her gods; return after your sister-in-law."

16 But Ruth said, "Do not urge me to leave you or turn back from following you; for where you go, I will go, and where you lodge, I will lodge. Your people shall be my people, and your God, my God.

17 "Where you die, I will die, and there I will be buried. Thus may the LORD do to me, and worse, if anything but death parts you and me."

18 *When she saw that she was determined to go with her, she said no more to her.*

19 *So they both went until they came to Bethlehem. And when they had come to Bethlehem, all the city was stirred because of them, and the women said, "Is this Naomi?"*

20 *She said to them, "Do not call me Naomi; call me Mara, for the Almighty has dealt very bitterly with me.*

21 *"I went out full, but the LORD has brought me back empty. Why do you call me Naomi, since the LORD has witnessed against me and the Almighty has afflicted me?"*

22 *So Naomi returned, and with her Ruth the Moabitess, her daughter-in-law, who returned from the land of Moab. And they came to Bethlehem at the beginning of barley harvest.*

DISCUSS with your GROUP or PONDER on your own . . .

When and where does the account of Ruth and Naomi take place?

Describe Naomi.

Describe Ruth.

How would you characterize the relationship between these two women?

What do you remember about Moab from Judges 3?

What did you learn about the LORD in Ruth 1?

How does Naomi view the LORD? What does she say about Him? What do you think about her assessment? Do you relate with her? Explain.

Describe Ruth's relationship with the LORD. Note specifically what she says in verse 16.

How does Ruth's faith compare to other people's you met in the book of Judges? Pick one or two to consider and discuss. How does her faith compare with yours?

Finally, what did you learn by marking the word "return"? Who returns, where and why?

OBSERVE the TEXT of SCRIPTURE

READ Ruth 2 and **MARK** every reference to *Boaz*.

Ruth 2

1 Now Naomi had a kinsman of her husband, a man of great wealth,
   of the family of Elimelech, whose name was Boaz.

2 And Ruth the Moabitess said to Naomi, "Please let me go to the
   field and glean among the ears of grain after one in whose sight I
   may find favor." And she said to her, "Go, my daughter."

3 So she departed and went and gleaned in the field after the
   reapers; and she happened to come to the portion of the field
   belonging to Boaz, who was of the family of Elimelech.

4 Now behold, Boaz came from Bethlehem and said to the reapers,
   "May the LORD be with you." And they said to him, "May the LORD
   bless you."

5 Then Boaz said to his servant who was in charge of the reapers,
   "Whose young woman is this?"

6 The servant in charge of the reapers replied, "She is the young
   Moabite woman who returned with Naomi from the land of Moab.

7 "And she said, 'Please let me glean and gather after the reapers
   among the sheaves.' Thus she came and has remained from the
   morning until now; she has been sitting in the house for a little
   while."

8 Then Boaz said to Ruth, "Listen carefully, my daughter. Do not go
   to glean in another field; furthermore, do not go on from this one,
   but stay here with my maids.

9 "Let your eyes be on the field which they reap, and go after them.
   Indeed, I have commanded the servants not to touch you. When
   you are thirsty, go to the water jars and drink from what the
   servants draw."

10 Then she fell on her face, bowing to the ground and said to him,
   "Why have I found favor in your sight that you should take notice
   of me, since I am a foreigner?"

11 Boaz replied to her, "All that you have done for your mother-in-law
   after the death of your husband has been fully reported to me,
   and how you left your father and your mother and the land of your
   birth, and came to a people that you did not previously know.

ONE STEP FURTHER:

Same Word, Different Translations

Take note of the word translated "wings" in Ruth 2:12. The same word (Hebrew: *kanaph*) will show up in Ruth 3:9 translated as "covering." If you have some extra time, see how else this word is used in the Old Testament, particularly in the Psalms. Then record what you discover below.

12 *"May the LORD reward your work, and your wages be full from the LORD, the God of Israel, under whose wings you have come to seek refuge."*

13 *Then she said, "I have found favor in your sight, my lord, for you have comforted me and indeed have spoken kindly to your maidservant, though I am not like one of your maidservants."*

14 *At mealtime Boaz said to her, "Come here, that you may eat of the bread and dip your piece of bread in the vinegar." So she sat beside the reapers; and he served her roasted grain, and she ate and was satisfied and had some left.*

15 *When she rose to glean, Boaz commanded his servants, saying, "Let her glean even among the sheaves, and do not insult her.*

16 *"Also you shall purposely pull out for her some grain from the bundles and leave it that she may glean, and do not rebuke her."*

17 *So she gleaned in the field until evening. Then she beat out what she had gleaned, and it was about an ephah of barley.*

18 *She took it up and went into the city, and her mother-in-law saw what she had gleaned. She also took it out and gave Naomi what she had left after she was satisfied.*

19 *Her mother-in-law then said to her, "Where did you glean today and where did you work? May he who took notice of you be blessed." So she told her mother-in-law with whom she had worked and said, "The name of the man with whom I worked today is Boaz."*

20 Naomi said to her daughter-in-law, "May he be blessed of the LORD who has not withdrawn his kindness to the living and to the dead." Again Naomi said to her, "The man is our relative, he is one of our closest relatives."

21 Then Ruth the Moabitess said, "Furthermore, he said to me, 'You should stay close to my servants until they have finished all my harvest.' "

22 Naomi said to Ruth her daughter-in-law, "It is good, my daughter, that you go out with his maids, so that others do not fall upon you in another field."

23 So she stayed close by the maids of Boaz in order to glean until the end of the barley harvest and the wheat harvest. And she lived with her mother-in-law.

DISCUSS with your GROUP or PONDER on your own . . .

What did you learn about Boaz in Ruth 2? Describe him.

Compare Boaz's instructions regarding Ruth and others' behavior toward her with the treatment of women in Judges 19-21.

Boaz Toward Ruth	Men Toward Women in Judges 19–21

What specific threats does Boaz note and address that are consistent with what we've seen in Judges?

What additional information did you learn about Ruth in chapter 2?

OBSERVE the TEXT of SCRIPTURE

I know this will be hard, but we're going to stick with overview and general comparison questions. If you'd like to study Ruth further and the topic of kinsman redeemer in particular, check out Precept's *Kinsman Redeemer*. It's one of my favorite studies!

READ Ruth 3 and **MARK** the word *covering*. Then **MARK** all instances of *redeem* and *close relative* in the same way.

Ruth 3

1   Then Naomi her mother-in-law said to her, "My daughter, shall I not seek security for you, that it may be well with you?

2   "Now is not Boaz our kinsman, with whose maids you were? Behold, he winnows barley at the threshing floor tonight.

3   "Wash yourself therefore, and anoint yourself and put on your best clothes, and go down to the threshing floor; but do not make yourself known to the man until he has finished eating and drinking.

4   "It shall be when he lies down, that you shall notice the place where he lies, and you shall go and uncover his feet and lie down; then he will tell you what you shall do."

5   She said to her, "All that you say I will do."

6   So she went down to the threshing floor and did according to all that her mother-in-law had commanded her.

Close Relatives are Redeemers

You may be wondering why we're marking "close relative" and "redeem" the same way. Here's the reason: they are both translations from the Hebrew root *gaal* which means to redeem, to buy back, to act as a redeemer. Kinsman redeemers bought back land for relatives in need and bore responsibility to avenge blood (Numbers 35). At times they also saved relatives who had sold themselves by buying them out of slavery (Leviticus 25:47-49).

7 When Boaz had eaten and drunk and his heart was merry, he went to lie down at the end of the heap of grain; and she came secretly, and uncovered his feet and lay down.

8 It happened in the middle of the night that the man was startled and bent forward; and behold, a woman was lying at his feet.

9 He said, "Who are you?" And she answered, "I am Ruth your maid. So spread your covering over your maid, for you are a close relative."

10 Then he said, "May you be blessed of the LORD, my daughter. You have shown your last kindness to be better than the first by not going after young men, whether poor or rich.

11 "Now, my daughter, do not fear. I will do for you whatever you ask, for all my people in the city know that you are a woman of excellence.

12 "Now it is true I am a close relative; however, there is a relative closer than I.

13 "Remain this night, and when morning comes, if he will redeem you, good; let him redeem you. But if he does not wish to redeem you, then I will redeem you, as the LORD lives. Lie down until morning."

14 So she lay at his feet until morning and rose before one could recognize another; and he said, "Let it not be known that the woman came to the threshing floor."

15 Again he said, "Give me the cloak that is on you and hold it." So she held it, and he measured six measures of barley and laid it on her. Then she went into the city.

16 When she came to her mother-in-law, she said, "How did it go, my daughter?" And she told her all that the man had done for her.

17 She said, "These six measures of barley he gave to me, for he said, 'Do not go to your mother-in-law empty-handed.' "

18 Then she said, "Wait, my daughter, until you know how the matter turns out; for the man will not rest until he has settled it today."

DISCUSS with your GROUP or PONDER on your own . . .

Why does Ruth need a redeemer?

How does Naomi try to help? What does she instruct Ruth to do? What risks did Ruth assume following Naomi's instructions?

What does Ruth ask Boaz to do and why? As you answer, compare Ruth 2:12 and 3:9.

How does Boaz respond? Again, compare Boaz's behavior toward Ruth with the way woman were treated in Judges 19-21.

Boaz Toward Ruth	Men Toward Women in Judges 19–21

DIGGING DEEPER
The Ultimate Deliverer and Redeemer!

Don't miss this Digging Deeper section!

The account of Ruth and Naomi touches hearts. It's a love story between Ruth and Boaz, it's a friendship love story between Ruth and Naomi, and it pictures the ultimate love story—God sending His Son to be the true Deliverer and Kinsman Redeemer for mankind.

Old Testament Roots
Scripture characterizes God as Redeemer throughout the Old Testament. I'll start you off with two references, but look for others to add that show God redeeming His people. Both the Psalms and Isaiah in particular use rich redemption language. The Hebrew root you'll be searching for is: *gaal*.

Exodus 6:6

Job 19:25

Others I found:

This is what I've learned about God as Redeemer . . .

New Testament Fulfillment
Now, take some time to examine redemption in the New Testament. As you do,
remember what you've learned about God as Redeemer in the Old Testament,
consider what Jews are looking for during the first century, and then see how
Jesus redeems.

Again, I'll start you off with a few verses to look at (be sure to read the
contexts, too) and then you can look for others on your own. The Greek root
you'll be looking for is: *lutron.*

Luke 2:38 (read verses 21-38)

Luke 24:21 (read verses 13-21)

Ephesians 1:7

Titus 2:11-14

Hebrews 2:14-18 (the word "redeem" [*lutron*] doesn't appear in this passage,
but the concept of redemption does)

Others I found:

This is what I've learned about Jesus as Redeemer . . .

OBSERVE the TEXT of SCRIPTURE

READ Ruth 4 and again **MARK** every reference to *close/closest relative* and *redeem/redeemer*.

Ruth 4

1 Now Boaz went up to the gate and sat down there, and behold, the close relative of whom Boaz spoke was passing by, so he said, "Turn aside, friend, sit down here." And he turned aside and sat down.

2 He took ten men of the elders of the city and said, "Sit down here." So they sat down.

3 Then he said to the closest relative, "Naomi, who has come back from the land of Moab, has to sell the piece of land which belonged to our brother Elimelech.

4 "So I thought to inform you, saying, 'Buy it before those who are sitting here, and before the elders of my people. If you will redeem it, redeem it; but if not, tell me that I may know; for there is no one but you to redeem it, and I am after you.' " And he said, "I will redeem it."

5 Then Boaz said, "On the day you buy the field from the hand of Naomi, you must also acquire Ruth the Moabitess, the widow of the deceased, in order to raise up the name of the deceased on his inheritance."

6 The closest relative said, "I cannot redeem it for myself, because I would jeopardize my own inheritance. Redeem it for yourself; you may have my right of redemption, for I cannot redeem it."

7 Now this was the custom in former times in Israel concerning the redemption and the exchange of land to confirm any matter: a man removed his sandal and gave it to another; and this was the manner of attestation in Israel.

8 So the closest relative said to Boaz, "Buy it for yourself." And he removed his sandal.

9 Then Boaz said to the elders and all the people, "You are witnesses today that I have bought from the hand of Naomi all that belonged to Elimelech and all that belonged to Chilion and Mahlon.

10 *"Moreover, I have acquired Ruth the Moabitess, the widow of Mahlon, to be my wife in order to raise up the name of the deceased on his inheritance, so that the name of the deceased will not be cut off from his brothers or from the court of his birth place; you are witnesses today."*

11 *All the people who were in the court, and the elders, said, "We are witnesses. May the LORD make the woman who is coming into your home like Rachel and Leah, both of whom built the house of Israel; and may you achieve wealth in Ephrathah and become famous in Bethlehem.*

12 *"Moreover, may your house be like the house of Perez whom Tamar bore to Judah, through the offspring which the LORD will give you by this young woman."*

13 *So Boaz took Ruth, and she became his wife, and he went in to her. And the LORD enabled her to conceive, and she gave birth to a son.*

14 *Then the women said to Naomi, "Blessed is the LORD who has not left you without a redeemer today, and may his name become famous in Israel.*

15 *"May he also be to you a restorer of life and a sustainer of your old age; for your daughter-in-law, who loves you and is better to you than seven sons, has given birth to him."*

16 *Then Naomi took the child and laid him in her lap, and became his nurse.*

17 *The neighbor women gave him a name, saying, "A son has been born to Naomi!" So they named him Obed. He is the father of Jesse, the father of David.*

18 *Now these are the generations of Perez: to Perez was born Hezron,*

19 *and to Hezron was born Ram, and to Ram, Amminadab,*

20 *and to Amminadab was born Nahshon, and to Nahshon, Salmon,*

21 *and to Salmon was born Boaz, and to Boaz, Obed,*

22 *and to Obed was born Jesse, and to Jesse, David.*

DISCUSS with your GROUP or PONDER on your own . . .

What does Boaz do for Ruth in chapter 4? What implications does this have for her and Naomi?

What did you learn by marking the words *close/close relative* and *redeem/ redeemer*?

Now, compare the genealogy in Ruth 4:17-22 with the genealogy you looked at from Matthew and record your observations.

What difference did a sovereign God and a willing kinsman redeemer make in the lives of Ruth and Naomi?

@THE END OF THE DAY . . .

As we conclude our time together in this study, prayerfully consider what you've learned and how you will remember and apply it.

Which person from the time of the judges most resonated with you? Why?

What temptations and dangers did you learn to guard against from the accounts in Judges and/or Ruth?

What key truths from Judges/Ruth will you apply in your life going forward? Take a moment to write your response in the form of a prayer, asking God to power your obedience by His Spirit.

On days when the darkness seems overwhelming and hope seems lost, remember that your God is a Redeemer!

"Let the words of my mouth and the meditation of my heart
Be acceptable in Your sight,
O LORD, my rock and my Redeemer."

—Psalm 19:14

EXTRA

MEMORIZE | TWEET | POST | DRAW | HASHTAG | ENCODE | REMEMBER

Let's finish strong by choosing how to remember the bright spot during the time of the judges—the life and times of Ruth and Boaz!

Pick and Memorize a Key Verse for Each Chapter

Ruth 1

Ruth 2

Ruth 3

Ruth 4

"Tweet" It

Summarize the message of Ruth 1 in 140 characters or less.

Summarize the message of Ruth 2 in 140 characters or less.

Summarize the message of Ruth 3 in 140 characters or less.

Summarize the message of Ruth 4 in 140 characters or less.

#Hashtag It

Write a #hashtag for Ruth 1.

#

Write a #hashtag for Ruth 2.

#

Write a #hashtag for Ruth 3.

#

Write a #hashtag for Ruth 4.

#

Apply It!

Summarize in one sentence what you've learned and what you will apply from studying the times of the Judges.

Now, try it in one word or with a short #hashtag.

RESOURCES

Helpful Study Tools

How to Study Your Bible
Eugene, Oregon: Harvest House
Publishers

The New Inductive Study Bible
Eugene, Oregon: Harvest House
Publishers

Logos Bible Software
Available at www.logos.com.

Greek Word Study Tools

Kittel, G., Friedrich, G., &
Bromiley, G.W.
*Theological Dictionary of the New
Testament, Abridged* (also known
as Little Kittel)
Grand Rapids, Michigan: W.B.
Eerdmans Publishing Company

Zodhiates, Spiros
*The Complete Word Study
Dictionary:
New Testament*
Chattanooga, Tennessee:
AMG Publishers

Hebrew Word Study Tools

Harris, R.L., Archer, G.L., &
Walker, B.K.
*Theological Wordbook of the
Old Testament* (also known as
TWOT)
Chicago, Illinois: Moody Press

Zodhiates, Spiros
*The Complete Word Study
Dictionary: Old Testament*
Chattanooga, Tennessee:
AMG Publishers

General Word Study Tools

Strong, James
*The New Strong's Exhaustive
Concordance of the Bible*
Nashville, Tennessee:
Thomas Nelson

Recommended Commentary Sets

Expositor's Bible Commentary
Grand Rapids, Michigan:
Zondervan

NIV Application Commentary
Grand Rapids, Michigan:
Zondervan

The New American Commentary
Nashville, Tennessee:
Broadman and Holman
Publishers

One-Volume Commentaries

Carson, D.A., France, R.T.,
Motyer, J.A., & Wenham, G.J. Ed.
*New Bible Commentary: 21st
Century Edition*
Downers Grove, Illinois:
Inter-Varsity Press

Rydelnik, M.,.
Vanlaningham, M., Ed.
The Moody Bible Commentary
Chicago, Illinois: Moody
Publishers

PAM GILLASPIE

Pam Gillaspie is a passionate Bible student and teacher whose greatest joy is helping people learn to love and live the Word of God. Pam has authored more than twenty Bible studies and loves sharing the Word while teaching locally and online, speaking at retreats and conferences, and mentoring others one-on-one. She holds a BA in Biblical Studies from Wheaton College in Wheaton, Illinois. Pam and her husband, Dave, live in suburban Chicago with their Great Dane and love spending time with family.

Connect with Pam online at:

www.pamgillaspie.com

 pamgillaspie

 pamgillaspie

We'd Love to Hear From You!

Please take a moment to use the link or scan the QR
code below and share your thoughts in a short survey.
Your feedback will help us guide others as
they journey through God's Word.

https://bit.ly/DeliveredBookSurvey